STRANGE
KEY WEST

MATTHEW SEAN CASEY

Price: $12.95

ISBN 978-0-9674498-3-8

9 1295

Phantom Press
P.O. Box 4766
Key West, FL 33041

Collector's Edition
10 9 8 7 6 5 4 3 2 1
ISBN 0-9674498-3-9
First Printing November 2003

STRANGE KEY WEST

MATTHEW SEAN CASEY

PHANTOM PRESS
KEY WEST, FLORIDA

Photo: RobONeal.com

To My Family:
Mom and Dad, Larry and Jesse –
Thanks for putting up with all of
my strange behavior.

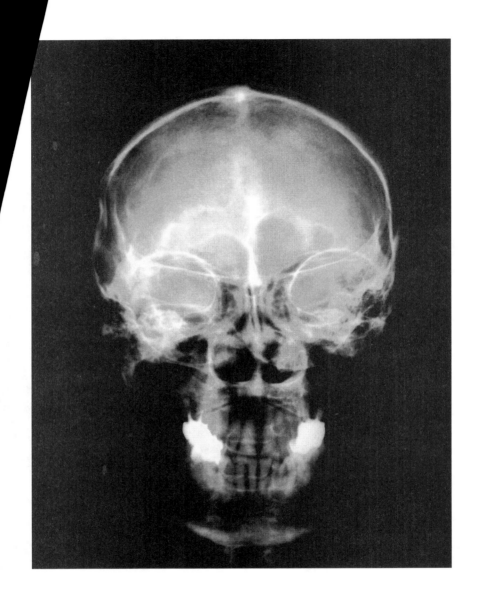

CONTENTS

Introduction: Define Strange

Define Strange. When it comes to Key West Strange, this is a daunting task. In most places, strange means something out of the ordinary. Where I grew up, strange was the next door neighbor who had a bat living in his chimney, the woman outside the library who got into arguments with herself (which she never managed to win), the old guy who walked up and down my street with an umbrella he never used, even if it was raining.

In Key West, this type of behavior wouldn't garner a second glance. To Key West residents, something has to be way out of whack to be labeled "strange."

The setting is strange. Key West is a 4 by 2-mile tropical island at the end of a chain of islands south of Miami. Before being "discovered" by Spanish explorers, it served as a massive burial ground for a tribe of Native Americans, the Calusa, whose bones are still found on the island today.

We also have an African burial ground. Two hundred ninety four freed African slaves died here in 1860 awaiting transport back to Africa. They are buried beneath the sands of one of our most popular beaches.

The inhabitants are strange. We've got a famous bar owner just off Duval Street who used to be the mayor. He also used to be a rum-runner. We've had people running around with dolls from the time they were children until the day they died, people exhuming and living with deceased loved ones, and people who make their living training cats to walk on tight-wires.

Heck, we even seceded from the Union, and not back around the War of Northern Aggression (that's the Civil War if you're from the North) either. We seceded in 1982 because the government installed a roadblock leading out of the Keys to deter drug trafficking.

It aggravated us that we had to wait in line for hours to get to the mainland so we seceded. Then we declared war. We surrendered (we didn't have any weapons of mass destruction) and requested a billion dollars in federal wartime aid. The check got lost in the mail.

We were, however, granted sovereign status. Key West is now known as the Conch Republic and we have our own Navy, our own flag, and our own passports.

The nice thing about all this is that it makes Key West an attractive spot for strange people. Most of the people who move down here were voted "Most Unusual" at graduation but down here we...er...*they* blend right in. And when you get an island stocked with strange people living together, interacting, and breeding, you get an awful lot of strange things going on.

Obviously I couldn't include every strange person, activity, or event in Key West in this book, or you'd be holding a volume the size of a small European country. So I have tried to select the stories without which the book could not live up to the title.

So settle in, sit back, curl up, and enjoy. Find out why locals say that Key West is where the strange turn pro. If this book encourages you to engage in your own strange behavior, blame as many of the consequences as possible on me. And don't forget to embrace the strange- we really like it and we rarely bite.

Desperately Seeking Elena

Nine years after Elena's death, her sister Nana began to suspect that the Count had removed Elena from her crypt.

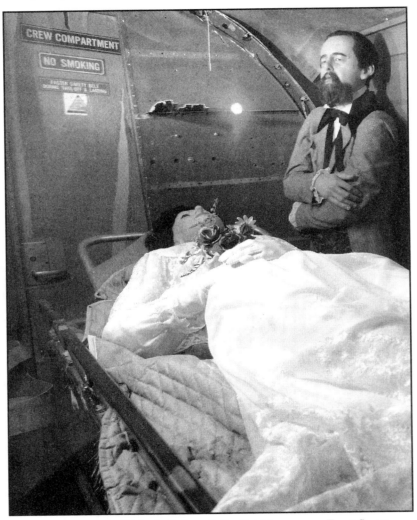

This display is in the Ripley's Believe It Or Not Museum on Front Street.
Photo: RobONeal.com

Few visitors leave Key West without hearing the bizarre story of Count Carl von Cosel, a man who lived with the corpse of his beloved Elena for seven years. When he was discovered, her body was taken away to a secret burial place. It is a well-known tale and has been featured in numerous magazine articles, books, and television shows.

Questions abound about many aspects of the story, from the Count's sanity to his preservation methods. But there is one question I hear far more often than any other in my job as a guide for the Original Key West Ghost Tour. "Where is Elena buried now?"

Let's start with what we know. Count Carl von Cosel was a self-proclaimed Count hailing from Germany. He left his wife and two daughters to start a new life for himself in Key West in 1927, and took a job as an x-ray technician at a local hospital. While working there, he met and fell in love with a patient named Elena Milagro Hoyos Mesa. Carl wanted to marry her but two things blocked his path- her husband Luis and her advanced case of tuberculosis.

Tragically, there was no cure for tuberculosis at that time and Elena died shortly before Halloween in 1931. Most people would have considered that the end of their marriage hopes, but the Count was not like most people.

Two years after Elena's death, Carl removed her body from the cemetery in the dead of night. He secreted her to his secluded home/laboratory and began an arduous reconstruction process. He started with her face, using mortician's wax and plaster along with glass eyes and a wig. He dressed her completed body in a white wedding dress, slipped a diamond ring on her unmoving finger, and married her. It was a private ceremony with no guests.

The Count and Elena lived together for seven years as husband and wife. The Count supported himself with the wages he earned at the hospital, but he also received a check each month from Germany. He told his friends he had owned a machine shop he had sold before moving to the States, and that the checks were proceeds from the sale.

The combined income allowed the couple to live quite comfortably at a time many were feeling the effects of the Great Depression. All manner of seafood was freely available in the waters surrounding Key West, and wild chickens provided dietary variety. Even after the Count was laid off from the hospital, his monthly stipend allowed him to purchase plenty of soap and cologne for Elena. That all changed in 1940.

Nine years after Elena's death, Elena's only living relative, her sister Nana, suddenly began to suspect that Carl had removed Elena from her crypt. After two confrontations in the cemetery, the second in front of a crowd of witnesses, Carl invited Nana to his home to finish their discussion in private. There he confirmed Nana's worst fears.

He revealed her sister, nine years dead, lying in his bed. He tried to rationally explain that he was merely taking care of Elena, and told Nana of his ongoing efforts to bring Elena back to life. Nana was not comforted by Carl's explanations.

As she left Carl's home with her husband, Nana insisted that Carl place her sister's body back in the cemetery where it belonged. The Count refused, saying that Elena belonged by his side. Essentially he told Nana that Elena would only return to the cemetery when they could both lie there together for eternity. Nana did not want to wait for the Count's death to have her sister laid to rest, but for some unknown reason she did wait five days before doing anything about it.

Police arrested the Count at his house five days after the argument in Carl and Elena's bedroom, and reclaimed Elena's body. Elena was put on display in a local funeral home where more than 6,800 people flocked from all over the world to see Elena. The Count never went to trial, although he was forced to undergo a hearing to determine the state of his mental health. The verdict: He was as sane as anyone else in Key West and was set free, albeit without his "bride."

The Chief of Police, an undertaker, and the cemetery sexton buried Elena's remains in an undisclosed location. The Count left

Key West for a rural south Florida town called Zephyrhills. Three hours after his departure, Elena's empty crypt exploded. The feeling around town was that he had dynamited it to show the locals exactly what he felt about their meddling.

Carl died 12 years later in his home. The sheriff who discovered his body also found an altar devoted to Elena and a casket on a long table. Resting inside the casket was a replica of Elena's body he had made when he still had Elena at his house.

This is where the facts end and the questions begin. How did the Count deal with the odor of his decaying bride? Soap and perfume. Did he have a bug problem? Yes. What did he use to rebuild her? Lots of things. Did he rebuild her entire body? Those parts that were important to him. Did they share a bed? Yes. And of course, where is she now?

One man took me aside after a tour and began speaking in hushed tones. I was a little nervous when he said he would give me $500 in cash and never tell a soul. Thankfully, he only wanted to know the location of Elena's body so that he could "pay his respects."

Most people have a theory about this, and most of them make a certain amount of sense. Some believe Elena was reburied just outside the cemetery sexton's office so he could keep an eye on her. Of course, if someone wanted her body, they wouldn't very likely try to take it when the sexton was around, would they?

Some say Elena is buried beneath the porch of the funeral home where her body was displayed the second time. My problem with that theory is that the second floor was used as apartments and it is also in a highly populated part of Key West. I don't think it would have been a very secret burial.

We at the Ghost Tour received an email from a gentleman who lived in a house the Count once lived in. The man's dog had been digging up human bones in his driveway. Keep in mind, bones are not an unusual find in Old Town, especially after a heavy rain, because of all the Native Americans buried here. My dog brings bones out from under my house every few weeks. Also, why would they try to hide

Elena in the Count's front yard?

The same doubts arise when people say Elena was buried right behind her empty crypt. Of course, I might have doubts about any location suggested to me because I don't believe for a second that she was reburied in Key West at all.

Key West may be a tropical island; but it's also a small town, and it's next to impossible to keep a secret in a small town. How people found out that the Count had Elena's body will forever be a mystery, but some locals definitely knew. A number of older residents say that as children they used to sneak out to the Count's house and then dare each other to look in the window at Elena. So why would this behavior be allowed to continue?

For one thing, Key West is a very tolerant community. As long as you're not hurting anyone, people really don't care what you do. Both of Elena's parents died a few years after she did, and her husband left her for another woman when she first fell ill. Nana was the only one left of Elena's immediate family. But the Count had a lot of something that most people didn't – money.

It probably wouldn't have cost the Count very much to ensure his privacy but it must have rankled him to have to hide behind his money. As far as he was concerned, he had done nothing wrong. He was merely taking care of his wife. In fact, he was trying to bring her back to life. He shouldn't have had to pay for privacy; he should have been revered as a scientist on the cutting edge of progress.

After seven years of hiding out, he may have decided to put an end to the bribes. It might also have been necessary to cut his expenses after he was laid off from the hospital. It would certainly explain why Nana waited so long to confront him. It might also explain the five-day delay between her "discovery" and the Count's arrest. Surely she would've given him a deadline to start paying again before she killed the golden goose.

Regardless of what you think of the Count's actions, it's obvious that he was not only highly intelligent, but crafty as well. He waited almost two full years after Elena's death to try to reclaim her body. He painstakingly planned the breakout and even had a dress rehearsal the night before he took her. It is doubtful that he would not have had a contingency plan in place in case someone tried to take Elena from him.

There's also the matter of the "replica" found in his house after his death. Why would he make a replica if he didn't know that someone was coming for the original? And why would he spirit away a replica of Elena when he could just as easily have hidden her away and left the replica for the police to find?

I believe that the count did just that. The police find the replica, display it, and then secretly bury it. The Count, after being judged sane, (perhaps a final bribe?) leaves Key West with all of his possessions, including Elena. He enjoys twelve more years of wedded bliss before he dies and the sheriff finds him with the "replica." This begs another question: What did they do with the replica/Elena?

We don't know, but while I may be a hopeless romantic, I like to think they just placed the Count into the casket with Elena beneath him and buried them together. It would have been the easiest means of disposal for them and the best the Count could have hoped for.

People will probably never tire of discussing this unique love story, and will probably never stop seeking Elena's final resting place. Regardless of where she is, the fact that there has never been a verified sighting of Elena's ghost suggests that she somehow found peace after she was originally laid to rest back in 1931. It's a good thing too because if anyone deserves a rest – it's her.

The Valbanera, as depicted on a souvenir postcard.
Photo: Courtesy of Monroe County Public Library

Final Voyage

*After her husband's demise, grief-stricken Mercedez tells
a reporter, "It appears that my husband may have had
a premonition that a tragedy was to occur."*

Captain Ramon Martin y Cordero stands alone on the dock in Barcelona, Spain. He gazes up at the 400-foot-long steamship that represents his third and latest command. She is the jewel of the Pinellos, Izquierdo & Co. fleet, the Valbanera. As of tomorrow, he is her captain. Standing on the dock, Cordero thinks about her previous voyage. It had been an unmitigated disaster.

The Valbanera had embarked on a 14-day passage from Cuba to Spain. She had been carrying 1,600 passengers- a full third over and above her maximum rated capacity. The wind shrieked as waves crashed over hundreds of drenched passengers huddled together on the open weather decks. They held onto anything they could to avoid being swept overboard. They watched the corpses of fellow passengers who had died during the voyage being thrown over the side even as they prayed for deliverance. Would they be next?

When the Valbanera arrived in Spain, an investigation was immediately launched into the behavior of the ship's doctor and her captain. The captain protested vehemently that he was being made into a scapegoat, but his protests were in vain. The owners terminated him shortly after his return and hired Cordero as his replacement.

Cordero glances at his pocket watch and sighs. He'll be shipping out in the morning and he's late to meet his wife, Mercedez, for dinner. As he hurries away from the Valbanera, he promises himself that her next voyage will be perfect.

Captain Cordero stands on the dock again the next morning, but Mercedez and their three-month-old daughter now accompany him. He holds his daughter in his arms, smiling as she tries to grasp the collar of his jacket. He converses with his wife as the final passengers make their way aboard. When he can avoid it no longer, he kisses his wife and daughter goodbye and strides aboard the Valbanera. He doesn't know it yet, but this is the last time he will ever see his wife and daughter.

The Valbanera's final voyage begins innocuously enough. She leaves Barcelona with fabrics and passengers safely stowed. She travels to Valencia, where additional passengers and freight are brought aboard. The Valbanera makes numerous stops at Spanish ports to pick up or offload passengers and freight. The voyage goes according to plan until they approach the port of Santa Cruz de Las Palmas, Spain.

The Valbanera loses an anchor en route to Las Palmas. Sailors are typically a superstitious lot, and the loss of an anchor strikes some of the Valbanera's crew as a sign of impending doom. Many in the crew are still haunted by the memory of their last voyage and the bodies they had been forced to dispose of. Coupled with the lost anchor, they start to feel that the ship may be cursed. The behavior of the passengers, however, is what causes the fascination with the Valbanera that continues to this day.

The doomed steamship docks in Santiago, Cuba, on September 5. The majority of the Valbanera's passengers have paid for tickets to Havana, the next stop on the itinerary. Even though they receive no

The wreck attracts fish and scuba divers alike.

11

refunds, 742 of these passengers disembark in Santiago. Most of their reasons for disembarking early will never be known, but their decision saves their lives.

The Zumalves owe their survival to their young daughter. Although she has been counting down the days to her first ocean voyage, her excitement vanishes as soon as she sets foot aboard the Valbanera in Las Palmas. Perhaps she catches the sailors' superstitious fear, or perhaps she has a bona fide premonition.

Her parents notice a change in their daughter right away. Far from excited, this outgoing and exuberant child has become withdrawn and apprehensive for no apparent reason. Weeping, eyes cast down; she refuses to reveal to her parents the cause of her distress-until they reach Santiago.

She pleads with her parents to leave the ship at once. Looking into their worried eyes for the first time since they've boarded, she assures her parents that the ship will never reach Havana. She informs them that the Valbanera is going to sink. Though tears continue to stream down her face, her voice never wavers. The Zumalve's relent in the face of their daughter's certainty and join the mass exodus.

Captain Cordero pens a tender letter to Mercedez before casting off the Valbanera's lines in Santiago. After telling her that he wishes he had a picture of their daughter, he writes, "In case I do not lose my life in this first trip, upon my return I shall enjoy the pleasure of my daughter pulling at my coat."

On September 5, the Valbanera sails into oblivion on a calm sea. In the Gulf of Mexico, a hurricane gathers strength and moves towards the port of Havana. The Valbanera is heading towards Havana as well, but the hurricane gets there first. The Valbanera's 488 passengers and crew are never seen again.

The Valbanera is a week overdue when the search and rescue effort begins. The search is a cooperative effort between Cuba and the United States. Cuban ships dredge their coastline, and U.S. Navy sub-chasers search the Keys, the Marquessas (a chain of uninhabited islands off Key West), and the main shipping channels- all without success. It is as if the Valbanera sailed off the edge of the world. How long will the fruitless search continue before it is called off?

The partially sunken wreck of the Valbanera is finally sighted in the waters south of Key West on the 19th of September, two weeks after she left Santiago, Cuba. Divers report that no efforts had been made to deploy lifeboats. No survivors are found, and no bodies are in evidence.

After her husband's demise, grief-stricken Mercedez, now a widow, will receive her husband's letter. As she reads and re-reads his final words she will wonder why he stayed aboard. As she tells a reporter after the Valbanera is finally discovered, "It appears that my husband may have had a premonition that a tragedy was to occur."

The Grotto.

Photo: RobONeal.com

The Grotto

*Sister Gabriel said a special prayer at the dedication ceremony.
She prayed Key West would never again suffer a major hurricane.*

The wind drives the rain into the walking couple's faces, trying to drive them back into the shelter of their apartment. Stoically, they turn off Fleming onto Duval Street, pausing to survey the main drag of their island home. Duval is almost completely deserted; for once there are no packs of teenagers racing rental mopeds, no sunburned baby boomers ducking into T-shirt shops in search of the quintessential Hawaiian shirt or straw cowboy hat.

"It's desolate," she says and he laughs. "Yeah, why can't it always be like this?"

They're still laughing as they walk past the news reporter from Miami who has stepped out of the bar at the La Concha Hotel to do her live feed. She glares at them momentarily for walking behind her shot. They can still hear her as they continue up Duval Street.

"Key West is completely empty of tourists due to Category 4 Hurricane Michelle, predicted to touch down on this island paradise within the hour. The city issued a mandatory evacuation order for locals two days ago but say that a distressing amount of the local population refused to evacuate to safety."

The couple moves into the middle of the street, holding hands on either side of the yellow line. The man is carrying a twelve-pack of Corona in his left hand; the woman is holding Scrabble and a cribbage board in her right. Ten minutes after passing the reporter, they arrive at their destination, a house on Simonton Street where a number of their friends live in converted apartments. Climbing the outside stairs, they can already hear salsa music from the second floor. The man pounds on the door, trying to make himself heard over the music.

Rob, one of the renters, yanks the door open and tries to hug both of them hello at the same time while simultaneously dragging them in to the apartment. "Welcome to your first Key West Hurricane Party. Make yourselves comfortable."

Rob takes the twelve-pack to the fridge as the newcomers walk around greeting their friends. Most of them are sitting on low couches and chairs in the living room, but a few are smoking cigarettes out on

This bust of Sister Gabriel includes a plaque inscribed with her prayer, "As long as the Grotto stands, Key West will never again experience the full brunt of a hurricane."
Photo: RobONeal.com

the balcony as well. The man does a mental count and comes up with fourteen all together, including Rob, Dave, and Terry, who share the second floor, and Al, Stephanie, Michelle, and Simon from downstairs.

In the far corner of the room, a 16-inch black and white television is tuned to the weather channel, but the sound is muted so everyone can enjoy the music coming from the stereo. Rob makes his way over to the couch where the newcomers are sitting and hands them each a beer. "How's the new place?" he asks, sitting down opposite them next to his friend Mandy.

"It's pretty good," the woman allows.

"Yeah," the man says. "The nice thing about the hurricane is that we've had two days in a row that we didn't get woken up by the

17

Conch Tour Train. If it wasn't for that the place would be perfect." In response to Rob's questioning look, he elaborates.

Pulling himself stiffly erect and smiling so that every tooth in his head is displayed, he does his best ultra-fake tour guide impersonation. "Ladies and Gentlemen, coming up on your right is -Mile Marker Zero. Two thousand, two hundred, nine miles south of Bumblebee, Maine, that sign gets stolen approximately 600 times per year. I don't know how thieves get those signs off; I'm just saying that if you came back here later with a nine-sixteenths wrench, you might be able to do something."

As Rob and Mandy laugh, the man takes a pull on his bottle and sighs. "It's not like I hate the train," he says. "I always send my family and friends on it. It's just that I hear every ten minutes, ev-er-y single day! I guess all those guys are holed up in Miami or someplace."

Rob shakes his head as he lights a Marlboro Light off the end of the one he's just finished. "Nah, they're probably havin' a hurricane party like us," he says. "They know about the Grotto."

Now it's time for the couple to look confused. "What grotto?" the woman asks.

"Oh that's right," Mandy says. "You guys weren't here for Hurricane Georges. The Grotto is over at the Saint Mary Star of the Sea Church on Truman and Windsor. A nun built it like 70 years ago and said that as long as it stood Key West would never be severely damaged by a hurricane." In reply to the skeptical looks she's getting, she says, "Seriously. You should ask Al about it. You know how he's in the Big Brothers/Big Sisters program? His little brother, Kevin, just did a report on it for school and Al helped him with the research."

"Actually, it was more like 80 years ago," Al says, walking into the room from the balcony. He holds an empty tumbler in his left hand. Al refills his glass from a bottle of Glenlivet and chuckles as he settles into an easy chair. "That report was awhile ago, let's see what I can remember," he says as he sips his single malt scotch.

"As I recall," he says, "It was finished in 1922. The nun's name was Sister Gabriel. She was a missionary from Montreal who got here just in time for the three worst hurricanes in the history of the island.

"The first two hit Key West in 1909 and 1910, and were extremely destructive. Since Sister Gabriel was also a nurse, she witnessed firsthand the results of the hurricanes. I don't just mean the people who suddenly had no place to live, I mean all of the deaths and severe injuries as well. But the worst was yet to come.

"The most catastrophic hurricane Key West ever endured struck in September of 1919. That storm registered the highest death toll in all of Key West's history. Of course, part of the reason the death toll was so high was because of a Spanish steamship that sunk south of Key West- almost 500 people died in that wreck alone. Sister Gabriel was heartbroken by all the pain and death around her and she decided to do something about it.

"She wanted to have a grotto erected on the church grounds with statues of Bernadette and the Lady of Lourdes. Everyone loved Sister Gabriel because of all the work she did on the community's behalf, and contributions poured in. The grotto is over twenty feet tall, with a recessed covered altar on the left side where people can light candles and pray. It's really beautiful- they usually have flowers decorating the statues.

"The Grotto was dedicated in May of 1922 and Sister Gabriel said a special prayer at the dedication ceremony. She prayed Key West would never again suffer a major hurricane. Sister Gabriel pleaded for God to protect the island's inhabitants from further destruction. She loved to visit the statue of the Lady of Lourdes and take care of it. Three weeks after she died in 1948, a major hurricane hit Key West and did almost no damage.

"Ever since then, whenever a major hurricane has been headed for Key West, it's always missed us somehow. Sometimes it turns, sometimes it peters out at sea. But even when it hits the Middle and Upper Keys, it never causes more than minor damage to Key West. Legend says that as long as the Grotto stands, it will protect Key West from major hurricanes.

"There's a pillar off to one side of it with a bust of Sister Gabriel on top. It has a plaque with her prayer inscribed, but I don't remember exactly what it says. It's something about Key West avoiding the full brunt of hurricanes as long as the grotto stands."

Al stands up and freshens his drink as the man and woman glance at each other, trying to gauge the other's reaction. The man is the first to speak. "Do you really believe that, Al?" he asks, trying not to sound too skeptical.

Al turns back to his friends and pulls a cigar from his shirt pocket. "I don't know," he says. "Let me put it this way, I'm willing to believe it." He looks as if he's about to say more, but Rob interrupts him.

"Hey guys," Rob says over the din, "Check this out." Rob turns the stereo down so everyone can hear the newscaster on the television. She's standing outside the La Concha again.

"Citizens of Key West are breathing sighs of relief," she says. Hurricane Michelle, a Category 4 hurricane that many experts predicted to ravage the tiny island, has almost completely missed it instead. The residents who remained on the island suffered only mild winds and bouts of rain. One meteorologist said that it almost appeared as if an unseen barrier protected Key West, and that the hurricane dissipated as soon as it approached the island."

Bone Island's Cemeteries

The 1846 hurricane brought a lot of interred bodies back up.
The hurricane also brought high winds, and a number of corpses
ended up in the branches of trees around town.

The "Vampire" crypt.

Photo: RobONeal.com

There are very few places in Key West that were never used as a cemetery of some sort. In fact, the entire island was originally a cemetery. When Spanish explorers "discovered" Key West, they found an island almost completely covered with human bones. The bones were all that remained of an epic battle between two Native American tribes- the Seminole and the Calusa. The explorers dubbed the "newfound" island "Cayo Hueso," which is Spanish for "Isle of Bones."

Eventually, the name Cayo Hueso was anglicized to Key West and the South Beach Cemetery was erected near the present day location of the Southernmost Point. Bodies were also occasionally buried behind (and beneath) various churches. Some of those bodies remain to this day in eternal rest. The deceased residents of the South Beach Cemetery were not as fortunate.

Key West is extremely close to sea level. This means that when we get a lot of rain, flooding is common and things beneath the ground tend to come up for a visit. Many homeowners in Key West continue to find bones in their yards after storms. A hurricane in 1846 brought a lot of rain, and a lot of interred bodies came back up. Unfortunately, the hurricane also brought high winds, and a number of corpses ended up in the branches of trees around town.

The city fathers, in their wisdom, decided to move the main cemetery to higher ground, thinking it would cut down on these types of incidents. In 1847, they purchased the Key West Cemetery for four hundred dollars. Although the earth is a bit deeper there than other parts of town, many bodies are now buried above ground in crypts.

The cemetery now enshrines more than 150 years of Key West history. It includes a separate Jewish Cemetery, and a Catholic Cemetery. The 300-foot Catholic section was sold to the Bishop of Saint Augustine for one dollar back in 1868. This is where Elena de Hoyos was originally buried.

William Curry was the first millionaire in Florida and built the house that is now the Hard Rock Café. He is buried in the main

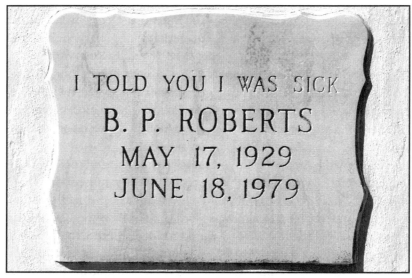

I TOLD YOU I WAS SICK

B. P. ROBERTS

MAY 17, 1929
JUNE 18, 1979

A well-known epitaph.

Photo: RobONeal.com

portion of the cemetery, not too far from the Porters. Doctor Joseph Yates Porter helped to stem the tide in the battle against yellow fever by quarantining infected patients.

A wrought iron fence surrounds the Maine Memorial which is topped with the bronze statue of a sailor. The memorial commemorates the soldiers who lost their lives when the battleship U.S.S. Maine sunk on February 15, 1898 in Havana Harbor. There is also a monument honoring 'los martires de Cuba' – the martyrs of Cuba. It reminds us of the brave men who sacrificed themselves helping to win Cuba's independence from Spain.

Speaking of soldiers, we have General Abraham Lincoln Sawyer. When his mother realized she'd given birth to a midget, she named him for the tallest man she could think of. She encouraged him to strive to reach his full potential. The residents of Key West were sad to see him go, but happy to grant his final request. They buried him in a full sized grave.

24

A town known for its colorful residents, many Key Westers carve their senses of humor into their headstones. Most locals can point visitors to the headstone of our local hypochondriac, which reads, "I Told You I was Sick." Rumor has it that her crypt face is fashioned from the nightstand she kept her medications on.

Thomas Romer, who served in the War of 1812, walked the earth for 108 years. His headstone claims that he was a good citizen for 65 of them.

One Key West wife inscribed, "Now I Know Where You Are Sleeping" on her philandering husband's tombstone. The headstone is no longer in the cemetery. Some people say it was lost in a storm, others say the wife removed it because she regretted the attention it was bringing him. Still others say she removed it after a confrontation with one of her husband's mistresses there.

The cemetery is also known for some of its non-human elements. Robert Otto, remembered for the doll he loved and lived with, also had a pet Key deer named Elfina. She is buried on his family plot, and a statue of her marks her grave. Three of Otto's Yorkshire Terriers are buried just a few steps away.

There's one resident in the cemetery who has been overshadowed by the fig tree he was buried under- literally. The tree actually grew around the tombstone so that now only a small portion of the stone can be seen. The tree appears to swallow the tombstone; it is known as the "Strangler Fig."

One tomb in the cemetery is paid for and inscribed, but not occupied. The inscription reads simply, "Wilhelmina G. Harvey (1912-   ). There is no death date, because Wilhelmina is still with us, providing a vital link to our past. She was the first woman juror, the first woman elected Commissioner, the first woman elected Mayor, and the first woman elected Mayor Emeritus in Monroe County. A born leader, she still leads parades in town and serves as the Admiral of the Conch Republic Navy.

A rumor persists that there is a Key West vampire residing in one particular red brick crypt. In the past, residents rendezvoused there on Halloween night before parties, but there have been no confirmed sightings. Most people in town agree that there is no vampire. Even so, it's not unusual to see crucifixes and cloves of garlic adorning the crypt it supposedly inhabits. And who knows? They must lock the cemetery gates at night for a reason ...

Voodoo in the Isle of Bones

*Some residents believe in the power of a well-cast curse
and always have. Voodoo is alive and well in Key West.*

A Voodoo doll owned by a Key West resident who believes.

Photo: RobONeal.com

Don suffered a stroke not too long ago, which left him dependent on a tricycle for transportation. When someone stole his tricycle, they robbed him of his mobility. He couldn't mount an effective search for it because of his failing health, so he decided to make the thief bring the tricycle back to him. How? He placed a curse on the thief and swore not to lift it until his property was returned to him. Did it work? You be the judge.

Police recovered his tricycle, stripped of accessories and repainted, a few miles from his house. Don placed the curse because he thought the thief was probably someone of low intelligence who could be scared into returning the tricycle. Some residents agree that the thief wasn't the sharpest knife in the drawer, and also point out the hard work of the police. But some folks in town believe in the power of a well cast curse, and always have.

Voodoo originated in Africa. Practitioners worship a host of deities, believing that each deity has individual and specific strengths to help their supplicants with specific troubles. Slaves brought the religion with them to America, but their owners did not approve of its practice.

Voodoo worshippers did the only thing they could to preserve their belief system. They changed the names of the gods they worshiped to match Roman Catholic saints and changed their holy days to match Roman Catholic holidays. The marriage of these two faiths is commonly called Santeria. Santeria is widespread in Haiti, Cuba, and many other islands in the Caribbean.

While many people refer to Key West as the southernmost city in the continental United States, others call it the northernmost city in the Caribbean. Either way, one thing is for sure- Voodoo is alive and well in Key West.

Marie was born in Key West in 1818 and lived on the island until her death in 1950. In her memoirs she describes Voodoo rituals – complete with animal sacrifice – that took place in a hall on Thomas Street. She also refers to packages found in the cemetery, which she claims are consistent with certain Voodoo rituals.

January 1989 – Jenny is enjoying a Sunday stroll on the beach with her Rotweiller. Suddenly the dog races away from her and attacks a plastic bag. The bag has washed up on the shore and is filled with a white powder. The dog has already torn the bag open and ingested some of the powder by the time Jenny catches up. The dog loses consciousness as Jenny cries for help.

The sheriff's lab technicians arrive and are unable to identify the powder. They rule out cocaine, flour, and plaster. They are unable to rule out tetrotoxin, a poison that causes paralysis and death. Tetrotoxin is found in the puffer fish that inhabit the reef just off Key West. It is also present in toads that are common in Key West. Voodoo priests use the poison to make zombies.

Once a person (or animal) ingests the zombie powder, they will lose consciousness. When they awaken, they will be a zombie and can be kept as a slave. Care must be taken when dealing with the zombie. If the zombie's creator is too nice to it, it will regard the creator as weak and attempt to harm the creator.

A zombie can only be made, however, if the creator believes in what they are doing and acts with full intent. This is good news for Jenny. Her Rotweiller makes a full recovery because no one was attempting to harm it in the first place.

December 1989 – Tommie leaves his New Town hotel at 7 a.m., dressed in sweats and ready for his morning run. He normally runs on the beach back home, but something about the beaches in Key West make him feel vaguely uneasy, so he's taken to running up and down Eagle and Duck Avenues. They're long, straight, and fairly deserted this time of day. He's on his second circuit when he makes his gruesome discovery.

Tommie kicks a crumpled up paper bag as he crosses 19th Street but doesn't stop running, thinking it was just a piece of litter. Then he sees the blood on his sneaker. He circles back, and what he sees makes him stop dead in his tracks. The paper bag he kicked has torn open. Blood spills out of it onto the street. Inside is what looks

A Santerian altar.

Photo: RobONeal.com

like a chicken with its head ripped off. There are other items in the bag, but Tommie doesn't get any closer. He calls the police from the nearest payphone.

The police find six headless chickens in a six-block radius. All but one are in paper bags like the one the tourist accidentally kicked. All six are found with chunks of coconut, kernels of corn, and coins. Police officially dismiss the case as a prank, even though similar objects have been found in the vicinity before.

The chickens constitute an offering to an unspecified deity. The idea is that people who walk past the offering will be subconsciously swayed in a certain direction, usually in favor of the supplicant. The offerings continue to turn up in this neighborhood periodically to this day.

July 1992 – Michael Dildy is a Navy Commander who has been stationed in Key West for three and a half years. Soon it will be time to decide between an assignment closer to his family in Washington and another four years under the sun. It's a hard decision, and he's pondering it as he leaves the post office and strolls up Eaton Street. As he weighs the pros and cons of staying in the paradise he's grown to love, he spots something on the sidewalk at his feet, partially hidden by bushes. Michael bends down to take a closer look, and gasps in horror. He calls the police on his cell phone and reports his discovery – a bloody human organ.

The organ is actually the tongue of a cow, which has been slit down the middle and stuffed with various objects. Inside the tongue, investigators find a handful of flowers tied with a gold ribbon, sugar, corn kernels, gold, a piece of metal, and a list of ten names on a card. The names include a defendant in a drug case, the officers who arrested him and others who had worked the case, three Key West judges, a Public Defender, and a parole officer.

The Santerian offering has been placed close to the courthouse in an area with heavy foot traffic. This offering has been made to appease the deity Ellegua, who likes sweets. It is worth noting that this offering is not the type that would harm, or bring injury to anyone. In fact, some think it worked in just the opposite way.

One of the officers whose name appeared on the card avoided serious injury by a hair's breadth the very next day. A woman driving a 5 ton truck somehow lost control of her vehicle. Her truck smashed into the officer's police van, causing severe damage to five other vehicles and totaling the van. The officer had stepped away from his van just moments before the collision.

Some folks in town believe that Ellegua was looking out for the officer's safety. Some, including the officer himself, do not. Like Don, his belief system does not encompass the supernatural. Just as Don was happy to get his tricycle back, however, the officer was certainly glad he wasn't in his van when the moving truck crashed into it.

Angela's Curses

Kneeling in front of her altar with chicken blood running down her arms, she raised her eyes to heaven and screamed, "A violent death to all those who have harmed my husband!"

Cabeza when he served in the US Army.
Photo: Courtesy of Monroe County Public Library

Hector Gomez waits patiently in his rocking chair on the porch of the house on Whitehead Street where he was born. His grandchildren pour themselves glasses of iced tea in the kitchen. Every year, about a week before Christmas, his son "Little" Hector brings Dave and Joni to visit for a couple of hours. He tells them stories about the old days when he was their age while their father goes out to buy a tree and bring it home. Hector knows they enjoy the stories he tells; but this year he's going to be telling them a story they haven't heard before.

Dave and Joni finally bring their iced teas outside and arrange themselves at Hector's feet, faces eagerly upturned, waiting for a story about a pirate or a haunted doll. Hector throws them for a loop right off the bat.

"I got a special story for you this year, kids," he tells them, looking each child square in the eyes. "It's kinda scary, but it happened right here in Key West. I know your Daddy prob'ly wouldn't want me telling you kids this one, but I figure you're old enough. But first you got to promise me you won't tell him I told ya."

The two children exchange uneasy looks. Poppy has never acted like this before. Dave is the first one to look back at his grandfather. "I won't tell, Poppy, honest Injun." Hector holds his eyes for a moment, then nods and turns to Joni.

Dave turns to stare at his sister too, praying his sister won't wimp out and cost him the chance to hear a "grown-up" story. Feeling her brother's intimidating gaze, Joni gulps and whispers, "I promise too, Poppy. I won't tell anyone."

Hector grunts, nodding his approval. "Good. Now don't you forget your promises." He sits back in his chair and reaches in his shirt pocket for a cigar. Hector scratches a match on the arm of his chair and lights his cigar, glancing at his grandchildren through the smoke. Both of them are sitting perfectly still, mouths slightly open, moving only to swat at the ever-present mosquitoes. Good, Hector thinks as he blows out the match and drops it into his ashtray, an old

The scene of the shootout between Cabeza and police.
Photo: Courtesy of Monroe County Public Library

coffee can. They look like they're ready.

"This all happened back in 1921. Christmas was coming up and most everybody was busy wrapping presents and trimming trees. But there were a few of 'em that missed out on the spirit of the season. There was this group of men planin' an attack on a bar owner. Before Christmas came we'd had our first drive-by shooting, our last state sanctioned hanging, and a voodoo curse laid down that's still going strong to this day.

"I'm gonna tell you kids about a man I knew when I was a kid your size. His name was Manolo Cabeza, but everybody called him El Isleno- the Islander. We called him that because his family had come here from the Canary Islands- he was Spanish. Isleno had himself a bar called the Red Rooster, kind of a small bar, but it was popular because he always had all these pretty girls around the joint."

Hector pauses, considering. Looking at his grandchildren, he decides they don't need to know how those pretty girls made their money. Hector drinks deeply from his glass of tea before continuing.

"Running a bar was a rough business in those days, people would drink for a while; and then they'd get to fighting. Well, Isleno didn't have too much fighting in his place. He was big, like a bull, and he wasn't afraid of nobody. Folks were afraid to fight in his place because they knew he'd get on them for breaking up his furniture. Believe me, boy, Isleno was one tough customer and nobody with a bit of sense would want him on their case.

"Well, old Manolo started keeping company with a pretty little girl named Angela who worked at his joint. The thing about Angela was, she was a mulatto girl, means one of her folks was white, the other was black. Now, most folks didn't care much who you spent your nights with, but when Angela moved into Isleno's apartment and started living with him as his wife, some folks got pretty mad. They didn't think people should marry outside their own color. I guess you've heard of the KKK. Well, we had us a chapter down here and they decided to pay a little visit.

"A couple nights before Christmas, 'bout five or six of 'em kicked in Isleno's front door in the middle of the night. They was all dressed up in their sheets and hoods and they started beatin' on Isleno with baseball bats. But he was tough and mean, like I said, so he fought back just as hard as he could. He even tore off a couple of their hoods in the fracas. But there was just too many of 'em for old Manolo.

"They got him tied up, dragged him to their pickup truck, and drove him out to the edge of town. They beat him some more; then they tarred and feathered him. They told him if he didn't leave town they was gonna kill him, but I guess they forgot who they was talkin' to.

"Angela nursed him as best she could, but he was in pretty sorry shape. One of his kidneys was split open, not to mention broken bones all over and bruises besides. Angela wasn't big enough to go out and fight those Klansman, but she got revenge her own way.

"She started praying to her Voodoo gods, and then she went out and got herself a chicken. She sacrificed it as she prayed, and then she put the curse on them Klansman. Kneeling in front of her altar with chicken blood running down her arms, she raised her eyes to heaven and screamed, 'A violent death to all those who have harmed my husband!' Her curse took effect eventually, but Isleno wasn't feeling very patient.

"How he got the strength to get out of bed I'll never know, we all thought he was gonna die in that bed, but he got up the day before Christmas and went looking for the men whose hoods he'd ripped off.

He was cruisin' down Duval Street in the back of a taxi when he saw one. Man's name was William Decker and he was driving home with the Christmas turkey in the back seat of his shiny new Ford.

"Isleno got the cab driver to pull up next to Decker's Ford, then he drew his Colt revolver and leaned out of the car, shouting, 'Decker!' Decker turned his head and found himself looking into the business end of a revolver. Manolo screamed, 'This is how a man kills a man!' Shot Decker right in the face, point blank and cold-blooded. Killed him with one shot.

"Isleno knew the cops and the other Klansmen would be coming for him, so he raced home. Sure enough, by the time he was locking the door behind him, the police had his place surrounded. As Sheriff Curry and Manolo yelled demands at each other, a mob of citizens and Klansmen arrived. The mob got under cover quick when the shootout started. The paper said Manolo and the cops fired over two hundred shots between them before Manolo surrendered.

"Isleno didn't want to surrender to Curry though, 'cause he believed Curry was a racist. So he surrendered to Deputy McGinnis instead, and as McGinnis led him down the street to the jail, we all cheered for him. He knew he wouldn't have gotten no justice out of the courts, and we were proud of him that he'd managed to at least get one of the cowards who beat him like that.

"McGinnis even got six Marines to guard Isleno's cell so he didn't get lynched. We thought Isleno would even get himself a trial, but we should've known better. Just after midnight, Sheriff Curry pulls up and tells them Marines they can go spend Christmas with their kids, he'll keep an eye on the prisoner from here out. So the Marines go home, then Curry goes home. Christmas day wasn't even an hour old when fifteen of the KKK showed up.

"Isleno's cell wasn't locked, so they just walked on in on him. He tried fighting again but fifteen to one ain't very good odds, especially when the fifteen have clubs and blackjacks. They beat on him for a while, took him outside, tied him to the bumper one of their cars, and dragged him out to the edge of town.

"They strung him up from a palm tree by the beach. I always figured that he had to have been dead by then, but they weren't taking no chances. They all took turns shooting his body with shotguns and pistols. Every man there had to shoot him at least once so they couldn't rat on each other. Somebody found El Isleno just after dawn broke, all beat up, mussed up, shot up, and hung up.

"Well, we all raised Cain cause what happened to Manolo wasn't nothing short of murder. I know, I know, he shot Decker first, but Decker had been one of the gang that beat him, tarred and feathered him, and threatened to kill him if didn't leave town. I ain't sayin' Manolo was entirely in the right, I'm just sayin' he didn't deserve to get murdered. Finally they got a grand jury together to make an 'inquiry' into his death. Course, we got no justice out of them, neither.

"When they got tired of 'investigatin',' they came back and said that even though Isleno got murdered, he brung it on himself. They said that he didn't belong in decent society on account of he was 'living with a Negro woman' and that his killers hadn't done nothing wrong.

"They must have thought they were in the clear, struttin' out of that court room like they didn't have a care in the world. Well, we were mad, of course, but we knew they weren't out of the woods yet. We knew about Angela's curse. So we weren't surprised when Isleno's murderers started having all sorts of strange accidents.

"William Decker was the first; of course, ole Isleno took care of him. That was our first drive-by shooting. One of them Klansmen got caught out in the Matecumbe hurricane and drowned, and two others went fishing and just plain disappeared. Their boat was never seen again either. One was a construction worker who was working on a bridge until he got blown up by dynamite that blew too early.

"Sheriff Curry prob'ly died the hardest. He was out fishing by himself over at the Dog Rocks on a flat calm day when he somehow got thrown from his boat and got crushed between his boat and the reef. I'm glad nothing like that ever happened to me."

Hector stops speaking for a moment as his son pulls back into his driveway. He knows Little Hector will be tired and want to get the kids home so he can have a drink and get some rest. Hector waves at his son to let him know the kids were coming and then turns back to his grandkids.

"You just remember this story when you think about telling someone else how to live their life," he says, leaning down closer to the children and lowering his voice. "Them men might've thought Isleno's lifestyle was wrong, and they might've ended his marriage, but Angela got the last word."

The Melting Man

When the cops asked Warren why he never told anyone his roommate was dead, he told them he'd figured Delaney was still alive.

Police were notified of a strong odor emanating from the house.

Photo:RobONeal.com

A 1970 Mach 1 Mustang, baby blue with black racing stripes and tinted windows, pulls up to the curb in front of a nondescript building. The driver's side door opens and Dennis Spillane steps out. He checks the door to make sure it's locked before pocketing his keys. As he walks around the side of the brick building that is his bar, he sees a man.

The man sits on a bench beside the door, head down, apparently waiting for him to open up. As Dennis approaches, he recognizes the man sitting outside his bar as one of his regulars, a contractor named Kevin.

"Yo, Kevin! What are you doin' here, bro?" asks Dennis as he holds out his right hand. His harsh Bronx accent almost overpowers the friendly tone of his voice. "We don't open up for like, two hours."

Kevin looks up at Dennis from beneath a faded Yankees ball cap as he shakes his hand. "You think I could just come in for one?" he asks. "I need to clear my head before I go home. You wouldn't believe what I been doin' today if I told ya."

Dennis shrugs his left shoulder and nods as he opens the door. "No problem, Kev. Come on in."

Dennis switches the overhead lights on and locks the door behind Kevin so no one else comes in. Kevin pulls a stool down off the bar and sits down. "Thanks, man, I really appreciate it."

Dennis steps behind the bar and grabs a Miller High Life out of the cooler. "No big deal, bro. There ya go, the champagne of beers," he says, smiling. He waits until Kevin has had a chance to take a drink before asking, "So what's up? What ya been doin?"

Kevin shakes his head as he takes another drink and then smiles as he looks up at Dennis. "So I get this call from this lawyer named Lisa yesterday, friend of my girlfriend, you know? She's got this house she's trying to sell but it needs a little work first, yeah? No big deal, she tells me, mostly she just needs me to re-hang some doors, patch some drywall, stuff like that. But she says there's also a problem with the kitchen floor and she doesn't know what to do with it.

The Key West Citizen, *April 30, 1992*

"So I tell her I'll meet her there this morning and we'll check it out. Well, I get there first and I'm just hangin' out on the porch waiting. But I keep smelling something, yeah? So I'm looking under the porch, you know, thinkin' maybe a sick dog or a cat crawled under there and died. Only I don't see anything. Then this Lisa shows up, looks at me like I'm half crazy or something. I tell her about the smell and she says she knows. Says the problem's in the kitchen."

Kevin pauses as he takes another drink of "champagne," emptying the bottle in the process. He produces a battered pack of Camel menthols from his shirt pocket. "You mind, D?"

Dennis shakes his head and takes an ashtray out of the sink where it has been soaking. "It doesn't bother me, man," he replies as Kevin lights up. Sliding the ashtray in front of Kevin, he reaches back into the cooler. He replaces Kevin's drink and opens an Amstel Light for himself. "So what happens?"

Tapping ashes, Kevin exhales a stream of smoke and continues with his story. "So she unlocks the front door, and bro, as soon as she does the smell gets, like, a hundred times worse. We go down the hallway and man – this place is trashed. Garbage everywhere, beer cans all over the joint, it was ridiculous. But the worst was the smell, man. It got worse every step I took. And then she opened the kitchen door.

"Bro – this smell was so strong, it was like somebody smacked me in the face with a snow shovel. I mean rancid. I'm holdin' my hand over my nose and mouth, but I could still smell it. Like sour milk and rotten eggs all mixed together, but something else too. Something sweet.

"As soon as I could get a breath and look around, I see all these empty beer cases stacked everywhere. The floor is hardwood and there's this white tape on the ground, like the stuff they use on T.V shows to outline bodies, you know? The part inside the tape is all stained. And then I got it.

"So we go back outside and it's a good thing because I was startin' to think I was gonna puke. I mean, the smell was one thing. But knowing somebody died there – right where I was standing – that was just freaky.

"So Lisa tells me the story and bro, I almost couldn't believe it. If I hadn't seen it and smelled it, I prob'bly wouldn't believe it. Right now I wish I didn't cause I have to go back and finish tomorrow. I spent the whole day there; I had to take out over half the floor. At least most of the smell went with it. I left all the windows open when I left, if anybody can stand the smell, they can steal all the empty beers cans they want for all I care.

"Apparently this dude named Thomas Warren owned the joint, lived there like fifty years or something. So one day he meets this cab driver named William Delaney, and they get to be friends. Well, eventually they got to be so tight that Warren invited William to live with him. In fact, not too long ago, Warren legally deeded half the house to him."

"Jeez," Dennis says, half under his breath. "This is startin' to sound like a Harry Chapin song." Both men laugh as Kevin lights another cigarette.

"Yeah," he concedes, "Well it don't end like any Chapin song I ever heard. Seems this cat Delaney was a pretty serious drinker, used to say beer was all he needed to stay alive. So one day back in late January or early February, he takes a spill in the kitchen. Nothing too strange there, right? Everybody falls over occasionally, am I right?"

Dennis nods soberly. "I see it all the time in here," he deadpans, and both men laugh again.

"Yeah well, turns out Delaney never got back up," Kevin replies. Warren thinks he just took a spill, no big deal, right? So he goes on about his daily business – for, like, two or three months. Oh, yeah. He steps over Delaney's body on the kitchen floor, every single day, for months.

"Then one day a service worker drops by and notices the stench about the place. So she calls the cops. Did I mention that the house didn't have air conditioning?" Nodding his head as Dennis grimaces in distaste, Kevin continues.

"Oh, yeah. So when the cops got there, they said Delaney's body had decomposed quite a bit. They said alcohol poisoning was probably the cause of death. But they weren't sure how the autopsy was going to go because, like, 30 or 40 percent of his body had melted into the floor as it decomposed.

"But that's not the best part. When the cops asked Warren why he never told anyone his roommate was dead, he told them he'd figured Delaney was still alive. Oh, yeah. Warren said he was pretty sure he'd seen Delaney stretch his legs sometimes and that he'd occasionally change positions.

"Warren also said that he used to ask Delaney things. You know, 'Do you want a drink?' 'Are you hungry?' 'Do you want me take you to the hospital?' Only Delaney never answered him. So Warren just figured he was being stubborn.

"The cops convinced Warren to turn himself in for psychiatric help, but I bet ya 2 to 1 they tell him he's sane. I mean, heck, it's not like he stole the dude's body from the graveyard like that Count guy, right?"

Dennis laughs and opens another High Life for Kevin. Both men hear a knocking at the door and Dennis realizes it's past opening time. As Dennis unlocks the door, Kevin starts taking the rest of the barstools down.

A tall guy with a shaved head and a goatee is waiting outside the door. "Hey Dennis!" he shouts. "How 'bout them Jets baby? You think the Dolphins are ever gonna win one?"

"Mattey-Matt!" Dennis says as the two men shake hands. "How are ya? Yeah, this kid Pennington looks like the real deal." Then he gestures to Kevin, who is just sitting back down. "Do you know Kevin? Kevin, this is my man Mattey, Mattey, this is Kevin."

As Mattey walks over to shake hands with Kevin, Dennis starts switching the neon beer signs in the windows on. "Hey, Kev!" he calls over his shoulder. "Why don't you tell Mattey the story you just told me? Maybe he can put it on his tour- or in a book or something."

Referenced Material

Undying Love by Ben Harrison, a novel

Ghosts of Key West by David Sloan, a novel

Sister M. Louis Gabriel's Prayer by Lynda Hambright, an article appearing in the Florida Keys Sea Heritage Journal, Winter 1993/1994

The Last Trip of Valbanera by Fernando J. Garcia Eckegogan, translated and appearing in the Florida Keys Sea Heritage Journal, Summer 1996

The Miami Herald – numerous articles

The Key West Citizen – innumerable articles

Referenced People

Many people helped me with their firsthand knowledge of the subject matter.

Tom and Lynda Hambright in the Monroe County History Section of the Key West Public Library were instrumental in my research; this book would not exist without their help.

Bobby Saunders first told me the story of the "Melting Man" and shared many a beer and many a Mr. Z's stromboli with me while recounting both his parents' and his own experiences in Key West.

"Diamond" Dave Gonzales walked the streets and generously shared their history with me until I could almost see them through his childhood eyes.

Fransisco, mi hermano Cubano, shared the tenets of his faith with me, simply and openly, in a way that allowed me to see Voodoo and Santeria with an entirely different mindset.

My eternal gratitude to all.

Thanks

There are so many, many people who helped me to finish this book with my sanity (mainly) intact that I cannot thank them all here. But there are some people without whom this book would not have happened.

First and foremost, David Sloan, my co-author. You've been many things over the years, a boss, a co-worker, a co-brawler, a friend, a drinking buddy, a traveling companion, and a confidante. When I hit the wall, you picked me up. I don't remember exactly what you said on the steps of 808 that January night, but I'll never forget you being there for me, as always. You are the man, Sloan. Stay Free.

The Ghost Tour Ghouls: Joni, Jason, Erin, Diamond Dave, Brant (Butters), Sara, and all of their families. Your friendship, encouragement, and support have been astounding, especially as the deadline drew near. You all honor your profession, and I'm proud to call myself one of your fellow guides.

The Jerky's boys: Dennis, Pauly, Tall Timmy, Vinnie K, and company, of course. The thrill may be gone (as Heather says) but the friends remain.

Mandy Bolen, the Editor. Not only are you from New Jersey, you were one of my first Key West friends. I remember telling Sloan "my half doesn't need any editing" and I shudder to think of the draft I left on your porch. I learned about writing by reading your notes. I humbly paraphrase one of my heroes, Ayn Rand: Does one appreciate perfection in editing? One recognizes it.

Rob O' Neal, the Photographer. If I had a nickel for every time I crashed at your house after a long night of close talking, I'd buy you a roast beef and cheese at Arby's. Your work was supernatural- even though I tried my best to sabotage you by conniving you into parking illegally, leaving your car unlocked, standing in front of mirrors, and letting my dog run through your shots. I hope you enjoyed the Busch Lite; too bad that guy didn't drink mojitos, huh?

Kerry Karshna, the design, layout, and cover artist (as well as my oh, so patient St. Patrick's Day beard dyer). I have a sneaking suspicion that you dye your hair to cover the gray I cause. You personify grace under fire, and I apologize for being the bullet supplier so often. ("Quark?" "Photo captions?" "Teasers?" "I think Rob has that picture." "The printer said yesterday will be fine.") You are a blessing, and your overtime heroics when I was just about ready to throw up my hands saved this book.

And last but far from least, Tommie Gunn (you call him Doctor Jones!) and Joel "that was a bit optimistic" Hall. Not only have you put up with more than a fair share of outrageous behavior on and off the field, you've been doing it for years. The first time I heard someone say "My brother from another mother" I thought of "youse guys." Germany 2006 – carve it in stone.

Discover Haunted Key West

If you are in Key West, be sure not to miss The Ghost Tour. Researched and created by *Ghosts of Key West* and *Haunted Key West* author, David L. Sloan. The Ghost Tour takes you through the shadowy streets of historic Old Town Key West where ghosts, ghouls and legends come to life. Tours depart nightly year round. For more information call 305-294-9255 or visit us online at: www.hauntedtours.com

About the Author

Matthew Sean Casey (Mattey to his friends) originally hails from Freehold, New Jersey but is now proud to call Key West his home. He can usually be found guiding a Ghost Tour or waxing poetic about "the good old days" when Jerky's was still open and there were no fast food restaurants on Duval Street. He lives in Old Town with Hannah Jane, his 1970 Beetle and Jitterbug, his albino Chihuahua.

HAUNTED
KEY WEST

DAVID L. SLOAN

Price: $12.95

ISBN 978-0-9674498-3-8

Inquiries should be addressed to:

Phantom Press
P.O. Box 4766
Key West, FL 33041

Thanks to Mandy Bolen for another genius job of editing.
Thanks to Kerry Karshna for design and layout.

Collector's Edition
10 9 8 7 6 5 4 3 2 1
ISBN 0-9674498-3-9
First Printing November 2003

HAUNTED KEY WEST

DAVID L. SLOAN

PHANTOM PRESS
KEY WEST, FLORIDA

Key West Cemetery.

Photo: roboneal.com

*For the people who gave me a ghost of a chance,
David L. Sloan III and Eileene C. Sloan.*

*In loving memory of
David L. Sloan Jr. and Michael J. Chadwick*

And for you Melanie!

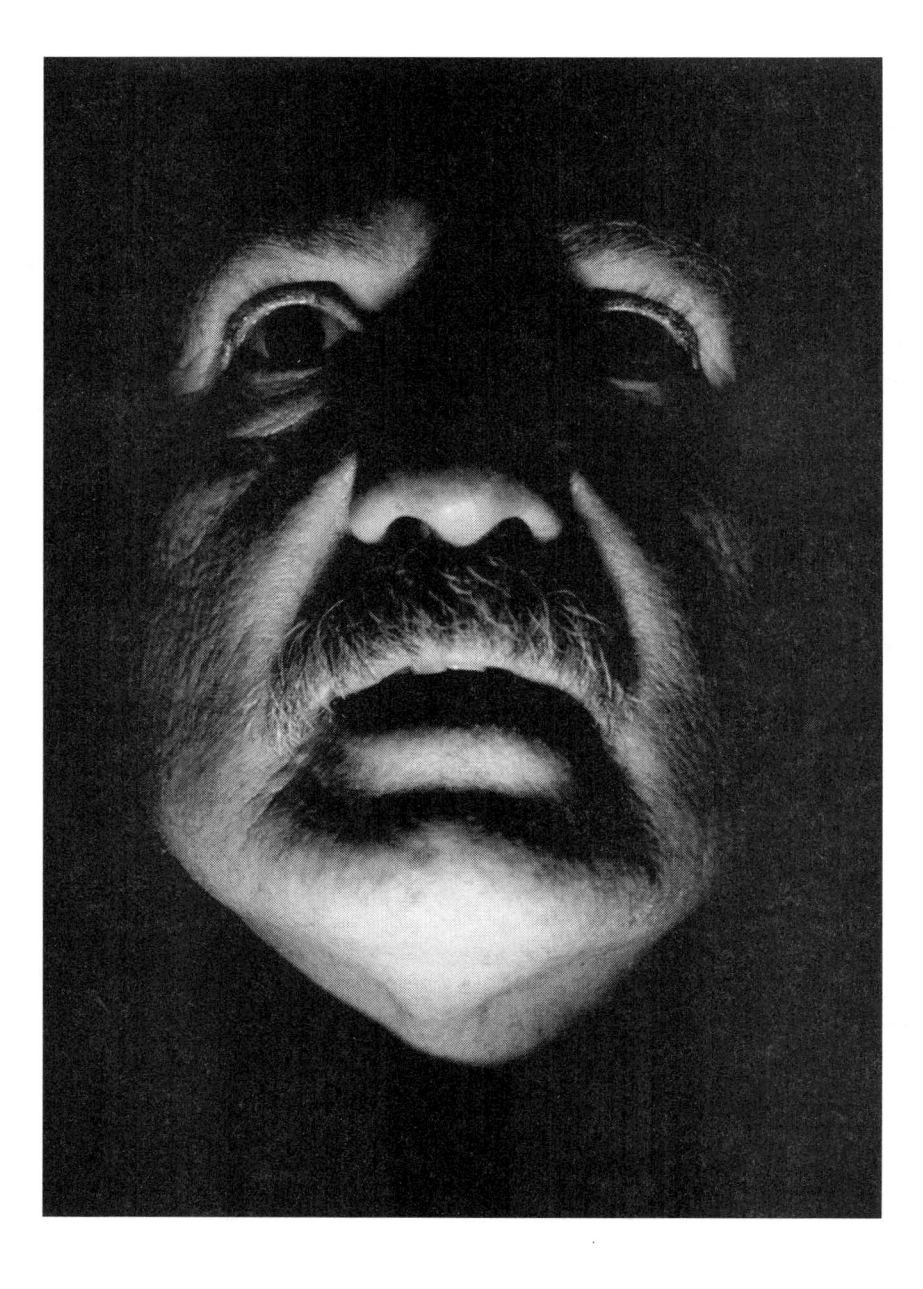

CONTENTS

PREFACE

When I first became involved in the ghost business I never imagined it would lead to a book, much less a sequel. Eight years later I find myself with more hauntings than pages in the book and the question of which ghosts are crying out the loudest for their stories to be told.

The existence of ghosts is not important. Some people will believe and others will not; it has never been my intention to change people's beliefs — I prefer to leave that aspect up to the individual and the ghost. Ghosts have taken the country by storm over the past several years with multiple ghost tours popping up in every major city and ghosts dominating the movies, print media and cable networks across our nation. Their stories are waiting to be told and more continue to unfold as we collectively become more receptive.

A favorite question of mine when interviewing potential tour guides for Key West's Original Ghost Tour is, "Do you believe in Ghosts?" Some do, some don't, and most fall somewhere in between. After a month or two of touring they are all believers.

Brant Voss joined us as a tour guide early in 2003. June was a busy month and Brant was conducting five or six tours a week, but it was the Fourth of July when he became a true ghost patriot. Brant enjoyed the afternoon snorkeling with his girlfriend Karen, but when they returned home to get ready for the fireworks and a night on the town he encountered a little problem finding his red, white and blue bandanna and matching shorts. They tore apart the closet and looked in every drawer and cabinet, but the items were nowhere to be found. Karen took the upper hand and told him to wear something else. When they returned home later that night the red, white and blue bandanna lay neatly folded on top of the matching shorts in the center of their bed. That same night Karen heard a voice calling her name; Brant was asleep, but their dogs Ralph and Alice barked hysterically at the mirror.

Every guide has experienced something similar and they have come to realize that the ghosts are communicating with them and through them to make their stories known.

The stories in this book are based on firsthand accounts I have collected over the years with additional information from the sources listed within the book. Most names have been changed as a courtesy and some situations created to better convey the events that took place.

Whether you are a believer, a skeptic, or something in between I hope you enjoy reading these stories as much as I enjoyed writing them. They probably won't scare you to death or send shivers down your spine like the big Hollywood movies, but if you think about them as you close your eyes at night you just might encounter one of the lost spirits that is trying to make their story known. This is Key West, and stranger things have happened.

The Lady of the Lane

Photo: roboneal.com

Appelrouth Lane is known for the popular bars serving up drinks for the masses, but stories continue to emerge about a different kind of spirit who is looking for more than a drink. The Lady of the Lane is only the beginning of a mystery that has yet to be unraveled, and perhaps never will.

Joe McGuire emerged from the nightclub and lit a smoke to conceal that late night smell that was wafting from Duval Street down Appelrouth Lane. It was another busy night at Wax and the mostly vacant lane provided a sharp contrast to the thumping beats of DJ Peter Worth and the throngs of people dancing to the rhythm inside. After selecting his scooter from the thirty or so parked outside, Joe turned the key, hit the ignition, eased off the kickstand and slowly cruised towards Whitehead Street hoping in the back of his head he would have more luck with the ladies at the Parrot than he had been having in any other bar that night. Little did he know the next lady he would encounter was the ghost of Appelrouth Lane.

Nobody is quite sure who this mysterious lady is, but unlike most ghosts she does not stick to one place, preferring instead to visit locations up and down the lane which is only one block long and nestled in one of the busiest parts of town. Her presence first became known at the Twisted Noodle, formerly the 416 and currently Martin's Café.

"We started out serving dinner only, so it was late in the afternoon before I came in to set everything up," explained Michael, a former employee of the Noodle. "The first time it happened I was stocking the coolers behind the bar when I noticed a young lady walking towards the back of the restaurant's patio. Normally I would have yelled that we were not opening for another hour, but she looked kind of cute, so I told her if she wanted she could have a drink at the bar. She didn't respond, and that's when I noticed she wasn't exactly dressed to Key West standards and she had a bucket in her hand. I thought it was a purse at first, but as I watched she headed back to the planter by the big banyan tree and acted like she was getting water

3

from a well. When she passed back in my direction I asked if I could help her with anything, but again she acted oblivious to me and just walked towards the front gate. I followed a minute later to see what was up, but as I reached the front gate it was still locked."

Michael and the other employees encountered their ghost on several occasions after this. Every account depicted a pretty young woman in a long dress walking to a well that was not there and fetching water in her bucket before disappearing, refusing to acknowledge anyone the entire time.

"We named her Noel, like a play on words for "no well." The most peculiar thing about her is she doesn't look like a ghost," Michael explained. "She appears like anybody else who would walk into the restaurant with the exception of the bucket. But what made things really strange was that when we were remodeling a few months ago at the Noodle, we tore out the planters and found the base of a well right where she was fetching the water."

Though the Twisted Noodle is gone, Noel has remained. People talk about a ghost at Big Ruby's guesthouse on the corner of Appelrouth and Whitehead and vacationers visiting Virgilio's have reported encounters as well. Tall Tim who works the bar at 420, behind Wax, told of his close encounter of the paranormal kind.

"I was setting up the bar on a Tuesday night when someone started banging on the door. Between the tourists and my friends there is always someone trying to get in early for a drink, but I was pretty busy so I just yelled for them to go away and come back later. The knocking continued and I was getting pretty upset, so I go over to the door and pull it open while at the same time giving a look to let whoever was there know I was not too happy with them. As the door comes open I see this lady crying. I ask her if she is alright but she doesn't respond. I don't know what is wrong with her, so I bring her into the bar to grab a napkin for her eyes. I didn't turn around for more than a couple of seconds, but when I turn back with the napkins, she's gone. It was a little bizarre, but this is Key West, so I don't think too much about it and lock the door back up, then I go to the bar and

start wiping down the glasses. I did the first one, set it down on the bar, finished the second one, and when I set it down, the first glass is gone. I looked all around and it was nowhere to be found, so I just finish up the glasses that are still there. About fifteen minutes later Vinnie K. walks in from the patio joking with me and saying, 'What are you doing leaving glasses out on the pool table?' He had found the glass I just wiped down sitting in the center of the pool table with a lipstick stain in the shape of a kiss."

As Joe continued his scooter ride down Appelrouth he noticed a nicely dressed woman flagging him down from the wall behind the San Carlos Institute. She wore a sad look on her face that indicated she had been crying. Joe slowed his scooter to see if everything was O.K. "Do you need a ride somewhere?" he asked. The girl didn't answer, but climbed on the back of Joe's scooter. He headed to the end of the alley and as they turned left onto Whitehead Street Joe cocked his head back to see which direction she needed to go. He stopped his scooter and looked back down the alley in disbelief.

She was gone.

Authors Note: Many of the people who work on Appelrouth Lane would love to know the true identity of Noel. If you have experienced anything ghostly on Appelrouth, or know of any history that would help identify this lost spirit please e-mail david@phantompress.com

Jerky's Bar

Photo: Rob O'Neal

A Stiff Drink!

Strange things were happening at Jerky's Bar on Caroline Street with no explanation until a bizarre discovery was made beneath the bar. "A Stiff Drink!" details one of the stranger encounters that took place in Jerky's.

Cody walked hurriedly towards the door with little acknowledgement for the turned heads and raised hands that greeted him. "Almost there." He told himself before rounding the foosball table and tugging the door handle. His nightmare was becoming a reality as the door refused to budge. Slamming rapidly against the hollow wooden shell with his fist, Cody let out a desperate scream. Bang, Bang, Bang. "Open the door, I've got to go out here!" It seemed like an eternity before the door finally opened. Cody wasted no time rushing in and taking his place on the throne.

Jerky's has never been the bathroom of choice when it comes to taking care of business in Key West, but Cody's options were limited with such short notice and he knew an ice cold beer would be awaiting him when all was done. Safely seated, his eyes wandered aimlessly around the men's room. To the novice it was not much different than any other downtown bathroom, but the locals were able to look past the damp floors and stained walls to see the beauty of this 4x4 box.

The slanted ceiling reminded Cody that a staircase ran to the apartment above and he wished he were standing at the urinal below right now, head bent awkwardly to the side in an attempt not to bump against the slanted ceiling. The urinal was probably the strangest Key West has ever seen, standing more than four feet tall with a marble base and single drain but the ability to accommodate two people at once while still affording privacy. Some old timers say this is actually the toilet that Ernest Hemingway took from Sloppy Joes, but people in Key West say a lot of things while making room for their next drink.

Cody's eyes continued to roam and his attention was drawn to the tiled floor. "What am I doing in here?" he asked himself and then realized he was not alone. A man in dark shoes stood inches before him, the tips of his shoes nearly stepping on Cody's feet. Cody's head jutted rapidly in an upward direction to find the suited man staring down at him with a confused look on his face.

"Get the hell out of here!" Cody yelled.

He was a strong guy, capable of taking on most of the bar if he wanted, but the stranger didn't budge.

"I said get the hell out of here!" he repeated, this time leaning forward in an attempt to shove the man back towards the urinal.

Moments later Cody emerged from the restroom and walked slowly to the bar. His face was pale and sickly as he relayed the story to Dennis, explaining that when shoving the man his hands went right through him. "I almost fell off the toilet and then the guy just turned towards the urinal and disappeared right through it."

Over the course of the next several months both of the bar's owners had their share of bizarre encounters. Pauley was preparing to open one evening while talking with a friend who kept glancing towards the jukebox. She began to get fidgety and her glances came with greater frequency until Pauley finally asked what was going on.

"Why is that man looking at us?" she asked.

"What are you talking about?"

"That man by the door. Do you know him?"

"I don't know what you're talking about, honey, but you don't need this." Pauley pulled Suzanne's drink away but could immediately tell she wasn't fooling around. Though he was invisible to Pauley's eyes, it would seem the mystery man had returned and decided to stick around for a while.

Larry Kaplan was visiting from Naples and came to Jerky's with his brother for some beer and billiards. One game of pool turned into five and it wasn't long before Larry headed in the direction of the men's room. Working his way towards the bathroom door, a guy walked in front of him going in the same direction. "I hope he doesn't lock the door because I really have to pee," Larry thought.

The slender man in the yellow shirt entered the bathroom with Larry following close behind him. Larry entered with his only thought being which side of the urinal would be delegated to him. The entire room was vacant; the man had disappeared.

Other ghostly guests began to appear, including an older lady

who stood quietly by the front door and watched Dennis as he closed down at night. She visited with such frequency that the bar patrons were convinced she had a crush on Dennis. She always came in quietly, after the bar was closed and after the doors were locked.

So why all this activity at one of the best local bars in town? Next time you find yourself walking down Caroline Street stop into the old brick building behind the Bull & Whistle and grab a drink at the bar. If you jump up and down you will notice the floor is hollow underneath. According to local legend, this is the pit where they kept the ice, and the ice is where they placed the bodies that were awaiting burial. The Key West sun can be torture if you don't keep cool, and it appears that some the residents of this onetime morgue are sticking around until last call.

Jerky's has since closed and the building is awaiting a new identity as this book goes to press. We hope the ghosts appreciate their new housemates as much as they did the staff at Jerky's. R.I.P.

The Watcher

Hemingway's first Key West haunt has a haunt of its own.
Is it the famous author banging on doors and watching people
from the entryway or just another lost spirit enjoying their
afterlife in the island of bones?

Casa Antiqua

Photo: Rob O'Neal

 watched with curiosity for several years as the tuxedo-clad gentleman led people past my residence, pausing briefly to point out the plaque reading, "On this site in 1886 nothing happened." His outfit was accented by a top hat and cape, and although we never spoke, I began to look forward to our nightly encounter.

Key West has always been dear to my soul. Her natural beauty, tropical climate and ample supply of unusual people strolling down the lanes create a magic that is rare. It was the people who first drew me from my room to the streets, and some years ago I began the nightly ritual of watching the world unfold from the comfort of my front door. I do my best work in the morning as afternoons prove a bit too humid for my taste, but as the sun dips below the horizon and sea air cools the island it creates a beauty that could never be appreciated from the confines of a studio. It has come to be that I spend the better part of each evening passing time from my threshold at 314 Simonton Street.

One evening, the tour stopped before my home for a bit longer than usual. The group listened attentively and acted oblivious to my presence — with the exception of one lady. She looked as if my being there startled her, though the others could sense that I was content to be left alone and listen in. People in Key West are pretty good at respecting the privacy of others. The guide pointed to the plaque but I was unable to take in his story on account of the look this woman was giving me. I silently excused myself and headed back inside, leaving my friend in the top hat to tell his story.

"Built in 1919, the Casa Antigua is now home to the Pelican Poop Shop, but the building has seen quite a bit of activity over the years. It has survived fires and hurricanes and served as everything from a flop house to a car dealership, and it also has the distinction of providing Pauline and Ernest Hemingway their first residence on the island."

"It was April of 1928 when the writer and his wife arrived in Key West on a steamer ship. Ernest was to pick up his new Model-A

from the Ford dealership, which occupied this site. But the shipment was delayed so the two were given lodging on the second floor above the garage. They stayed here for seven weeks and during that time Hemingway completed his first draft of "A Farewell to Arms." They fell in love with what he coined "St. Tropez of the poor" and remained on the island for thirteen years.'

The following night my interest was piqued as I observed my friend speaking of ghosts in the house. In all of my time here I have never seen a hint of such activity, but then again I am a bit of a skeptic. For nearly five years we had encountered each other on a nightly basis without speaking, but I felt enough comfort with the matter to play along. It was a Friday evening and though I don't know what sparked my playfulness, I ducked behind the door as I saw the lantern turning from Eaton Street onto Simonton. Standing in my doorway he spoke of the plaque, went into the history of my residence and then 'BOOM!'

I hit the closed door with all of my might, and judging by the screams on the other side it was quite a hit. My friend was so startled he had trouble telling his story, but I think we all had a good laugh about the episode. I'll still bang against the door on occasion, just to keep them on their toes, of course, but for the most part I'm happy watching. Perhaps tonight I'll listen to the whole story and see what this ghost business is all about.

"Though Hemingway does not live in this house anymore, there are those who believe his spirit still does. A few months ago we had a psychic on the tour and she approached me at the end to ask about the building with the large wooden doors. At the time I was not sure which building she was talking about, but the psychic explained she had seen a ghost standing in the doorway. 'He was a broad shouldered man looking blankly towards the street,' she explained.

"Several weeks later a college student from Iowa asked about the man in the doorway, and two days later a teacher from England had the same question. 'Can you show me the door?' I asked. She walked me back to Simonton Street and pointed to the entrance of the

Pelican Poop Shop. Since adding this house to our tour we have had a number of people see the man, and on occasion there will be a loud knocking coming from inside the door. Some say it is the ghost of Ernest Hemingway, but if George Washington had slept here they would probably say it was his spirit. During a time when the building served as an auto shop, there were some men who died when batteries exploded in the heat. The ghost could be Hemingway, an unfortunate mechanic, or one of the many people who had the good fortune of staying in this home. We don't like to speculate, so let's just call him 'the watcher' as that is what he likes to do."

That seems a bit peculiar. They're talking about me as if I am a ghost...

Hemingway Home & Museum on Whitehead St.

Photo: roboneal.com

Haunted Hemingway

The month of July brings scores of Hemingway fans and look-alikes to Key West for a celebration dedicated to the author's life and times, but some claim it attracts the attention of the author himself. Does Hemingway's ghost still yearn for the days he spent fishing in the Keys? More than one Hemingway look-alike and several employees of the author's home believe he does.

Six men gathered around the sturdy oak table that occupied the majority of the floor space on the drinking side of the Chart Room bar. Tossing back mojitos and cracking the salty peanuts before disposing of their shells on the floor, each man had a devilish gleam in his eyes as he crafted a story that would one-up the tale told before it.

"Another mojito!" Frank beckoned to the bartender while puffing his chest and deepening his voice for effect.

"Make that two!" mimicked Lenny, his voice even deeper than Frank's.

Not to be outdone, the remaining four men followed suit with the drink orders, each one puffing their chest and lowering their voice with greater exaggeration than the one before them. When the sixth man had ordered they simultaneously broke into a roar of laughter.

Valerie crushed mint, added sugar and rum and began working her way around the table placing a drink before each of the bearded gentlemen. "There you go, Ernest, and here's one for you Ernest, a mojito for Ernest, the same for Ernest, another for you Ernest, and last but not least, your mojito, Mr. Hemingway." They raised each glass to the center of the table and toasted the real Ernest Hemingway. These look-alikes were just brushing up for the storytelling competition the following day.

The drinks continued to flow as each took their turn spinning yarns about fish they had caught, girls they had landed or drinks they had drunk. When Frank's turn came around, a solemn look went across his face and after many moments of uncomfortable silence he spoke. "Turn down the lights, Valerie." She couldn't tell if it was a demand or a request, but heeded his instructions and allowed the room to be cast in little more than shadows. Frank grasped the Ouija Board from a pile of games beneath the television and placed its components on the table.

"You are all aware that the Ouija Board has the power to connect us directly with the dead, but you may not know that the dead

are already among us. Interred in the very bar on which the mojitos you are enjoying were prepared are the ashes of a man who used to frequent the Chart Room. Next to his ashes is an empty space reserved for General Chapman of the Conch Republic when he passes, and this is also the very bar where the late, great Mel Fisher plotted his discovery of the Atocha." The men looked at Valerie for verification of the facts as she nodded her head and pointed to the burial spot on the bar.

"Key West has always been known for her hauntings," he continued. "But earlier this very evening I came face to face with the papa of all ghosts." The men leaned in closer watching Frank's eyes for any signs he was lying. None could be detected.

"It was twenty-two minutes past eight o'clock when I approached the lighthouse. Crossing diagonally on Whitehead Street I was amazed at the lack of activity around his house, but relished the silence and welcomed it as an opportunity to reflect on the man we all love to imitate. I walked toward the front gate imagining I was him coming home from an evening on the town and could almost sense what he felt as my boat shoes shuffled along the sidewalk and the jasmine traveled gently through the air."

"I clasped my hands around the bars of the entry and stood for a few minutes gazing at the house. It was the first time I had been alone there and the sensation was invigorating. Just then I was distracted by a noise and noticed I was not alone. I cast my gaze to the shadow that drifted across the upper veranda, silently cursing the caretaker who had interrupted my solitude. As they walked into the light my thoughts went from anger to confusion as Old Man Hemingway appeared not twenty yards in front me."

"Now before you accuse me of losing my marbles there are a few things that should be explained. First off, I was not drinking. Secondly, there are people who work at that house who have talked about his ghost, experiencing everything from cold chills to the sound of a typewriter clacking away in the early morning. Thirdly, I've happened to notice that there are more than a few look-alikes wandering

the streets of Key West this time of year, and I'm anything but gullible."

"I figured it was one of us getting a special after-hours tour of the place so I called up to the balcony in hopes of joining in. 'Hey, Ernest!' I yelled and the man walked to the edge of the balcony where his gaze met mine. I waved my arm back and forth and called out 'It's me, Frank.' He responded with a hearty wave and then right before my eyes became transparent and disappeared."

"I stood dumbfounded for several minutes trying to figure out what had happened. Eventually gaining my composure, I turned to walk away, but as my hands released their grip from the gate an icy cold breeze blew against my back and rushed through the gate stirring up leaves on the walk as it headed to the front door of his house."

"The hair on the back of my neck stood up for a good portion of my walk down Duval Street. It only happened on my way to meet you here tonight. You may call me crazy, but do I believe I met the ghost of Ernest Hemingway?" There was another moment of silence before the men followed Frank's gaze to the center of the table. The glass cylinder of the Ouija Board's indicator rested firmly on 'yes.'

Ten Lives?

*It has been said that people and their pets have a lot in common.
In Key West it appears that the animals have taken after the humans
and decided to stick around for a while longer. "Ten Lives" details
one account of a ghost cat that haunts the Hemingway estate.*

The cat cemetery at the Hemingway estate.

Photo: roboneal.com

"**H**ow did she get in here? I thought you closed the doors before coming to bed." Nick wasn't angry, just a little surprised at her presence. "I did close the doors," Joan said. "Maybe she was hiding under the bed."

Nick and Joan lived at 907 Whitehead Street. The 1851 house is best known as the home of Ernest Hemingway, but has played host over the years to a number of celebrities including Charlie Chaplin, Ava Gardner, Emily Dickinson, Marilyn Monroe, Pablo Picasso and Mark Twain, just to mention a few.

Quite an impressive guest list, and it just so happens that most of the famous guests have taken up full-time residence where the famous author created such works as "Death in the Afternoon," "To Have and Have Not" and "For Whom the Bell Tolls." They are the cats, who along with the famous author, bring charm and grace to one of the island's favorite attractions.

Most cats have five toes on each foot in the front and four in back, but genetics and inbreeding can cause additional digits making the cats "polydactyl" in the scientific world, or simply "Hemingway cats" in Key West. Ernest was given his first six-toed cat by a sea captain, and many of the more than sixty cats still living on the property today are descendants of the original.

Hemingway owned the home from 1931 until his death in 1961, but spent less time there after his divorce from Pauline in 1939, when he purchased a residence in Cuba. The home was sold to Bernice Dickson in 1961, but only opened as a museum in 1964. It was during these years that Nick and Joan Di Lorenzo had the pleasure of renting a room above the old carriage house ñ the former studio of Ernest Hemingway.

It seemed innocent enough when it first happened. The two were lying in bed when a black and white tuxedo cat decided to join them. She hopped on the mattress between their feet and proceeded to walk across Nick's legs until she was comfortably perched at chest level. Paws kneading and motor purring the cat was in heaven. Nick

23

attempted to pet her but she vanished into thin air.

It happened several more times, the last being early one morning. Nick felt the familiar paws across his chest and opened his eyes to see the same black and white cat with her face just inches from his nose. "Yowrlllllll." The cat stared into his eyes while emitting the sound, faded in color until she was transparent and then disappeared without a trace, proving at least one of Hemingway's cats has more than nine lives.

Fantasmo de Finca Vigia

*Can our spirits travel back to all of our favorite places when
we pass on? Stories from Finca Vigia, Hemingway's Cuban estate,
seem to indicate so. Or maybe it is a special privilege
reserved for famous authors.*

Hemingway's living room in Cuba.

Photo: roboneal.com

La Finca Vigia may not be a familiar estate to many American's, but it is a name that brings fear to the hearts of several Cubans who were employed there over the past several years. Best known as the former Cuban home of the award winning author Ernest Hemingway, these employees believe his ghost is alive and well, and still residing at La Finca.

The estate is quite sizeable and spans several acres with a variety of trees and lush vegetation. Deeded to the Cuban government in 1960, the home looks exactly as is did when Hemingway was living there, with original furniture, hunting trophies, manuscripts, shoes, pants and boots that give the impression he has only stepped away for a few minutes. Tropical paths lurk about the estate and wind down the hills to reveal a guest home, swimming pool, pet cemetery and Papa's prize boat, the Pilar. It seems the paths are not the only things lurking around the famous estate.

Idania Rodriguez had worked at Finca for several years. She started at the gate giving directions for tourists and buses, but eventually moved into the guesthouse, where the job consisted mainly of making sure people didn't try to walk away with any of the Hemingway belongings. It was here that she had her first ghostly encounter.

"It was the middle of the afternoon and I was standing in the main room of the guest house. It is up on the second floor so the only way to get in is from the steps outside, and then you can only come in a little bit because I am standing there to stop you. There was nobody on the steps at the time, so I was just waiting for people to come when I heard footsteps in the room behind me. Nobody is allowed back there, so I ran back to tell them to leave, but the footsteps stopped. It happened two more times that month and the last time I saw the shadow of a man but no one was there. I told my boss I didn't like it there, so the next week they moved me to the main house."

Idania's job in the main house was still stopping people from

grabbing Ernest's stuff through the open windows of the house, but it also included preventing photos from being taken of the homes interior, or collecting $10 a shot. The main house staff also had the responsibility of locking everything up at night, a task that would soon lead to Idania's departure.

"Nadia was closing up the entryroom when I locked the windows of the bathroom and the library. I was standing by the shoe rack when I could feel someone behind me, and though I turned around, no one was there. I started to walk back to the main room when I felt a cold breath by my ear and a voice that whispered, 'What are you doing here?' It was a man's voice, but there was no man around. I told Nadia and she said it was just the ghost, but he was not bad. I was not sure I agreed."

Idania took to closing the exteriors of the house, after the whispering incident, but it seems nowhere on the estate was safe for her, or perhaps the ghost had taken a liking to her dark eyes and the curls in her hair.

"It was a full moon the night that I saw him and I was the last one still closing. I was walking down the path to the pool when I heard a stick break on the ground behind me. When I turned around there was a man coming down the path, a tall, red-faced man, walking slowly and dressed with Bermudas, a light, baggy shirt, and leather sandals. I started to walk away from him but he continued to follow. The faster I walked away, the faster he followed me. When I realized it was him, I went straight to the gate and left the key hanging on a palm tree before running home."

The Cuban Ministry of Tourism believes the sightings of Ernest's ghost will benefit Finca Vigia, but Idania Rodriguez resigned making one less person who will be visiting Hemingway's Cuban estate.

The Masks

The Salvation Army Thrift Store is normally a place to seek out bargains and find some great deals, but one Key West man got more than he had bargained for.

The masks.

Photo: Larry Stanford

"**H**elp! Stop it! Get them off me!"

Rob ran from his bedroom in a panic that had become routine over the past several days. Dave jumped from his makeshift bed in the hallway, making a desperate attempt to figure out what was going on. "Spiders – the spiders are everywhere – come look at the bed."

Things were pretty normal at 808 Simonton Street for the last year and a half considering three semi-professional men in their early thirties were sharing a three-bedroom apartment in Old Town, which seemed to become the epicenter of every late-night party they attended. Not that it was a house of debauchery; each had a girlfriend and showed up to work on time, but they enjoyed their beer and it made for some interesting stories, even by Key West standards.

The problems started in early March after Dave took a trip to Fort Lauderdale and picked up some masks from the Salvation Army. It was a Monday morning and the store was divided into various sections; Men's clothes here, women's clothes there, furniture on this side, kid's stuff on that side. The masks were hidden behind a lime green couch from the late '60s and came as a pair — one female and one male. They stood nearly three feet tall, hand carved from mahogany wood with sharp horns, pointed teeth and demonic eyes. The $40 price tag seemed high for the Salvation Army, but Dave had to have them. He picked them up by the support wires spanning the backs of their heads and walked to the register.

"Did you see what he's getting?" one cashier asked another who was placing shirts on a nearby rack. The question rolled from her mouth with a slow ominous tone that might indicate she knew something more, but Dave brushed it off as superstition. "Uhh-huhh." She replied, eyes glancing to the side and head raised as she looked cautiously down her nose at his new purchase. Dave figured they were just jealous.

Dave felt good about his find, as he hung the masks over his bed in Key West. He had never seen such an unusual carving and the price really wasn't that bad. That night, things started getting strange.

31

Dave had been sleeping with his door open so he could see the clock in the living room that hung above the front door. It was 5:00 am when he awoke, not with a start, not feeling tired, but simply awake with the sense he was being watched. Looking towards the clock he was taken aback by the image of a woman dressed in a Victorian hoop skirt holding her young daughters hand and peering into his room with a look of concern.

"This isn't happening," he thought, but the image was clear as day. Dave had not been drinking that night. The episode lasted several minutes with the daughter pulling on her mother's dress while pointing towards his room and the mother whispering in her daughter's ear. They eventually vanished, but it would not be the last time the duo paid a visit.

The following night it happened again at precisely 5:00 a.m. Dave was visited two more times before relocating his comforter to the space directly in front of Rob's room in the hallway on the other end of the house. "Maybe that will make them go away," he hoped. The ghosts were not frightening or aggressive but they made it a bit unnerving to sleep.

Dave, wrapped in his blanket, positioned himself on the floor and closed his eyes. A chill filled the hallway but he refused to open his eyes, and then it happened. A dark shadow began to descend upon him, becoming more and more visible despite the fact his eyes were closed. It came within inches of his face before his eyes shot open and it disappeared. He closed his eyes again and the creature returned.

Dave thought he was going crazy. "It's all in my head. None of this is real. It's just my imagination." He had almost convinced himself and was about to close his eyes again when Rob came running from his room screaming something about snakes. Things were not right at 808 Simonton Street.

And so it went on for several weeks. Rob was plagued by nightmares that included attacks by snakes, spiders, grasshoppers and even camels and Dave was visited by dark shadows and women in hoop

skirts on a nightly basis. They figured it must be the masks and moved them to a storage shed. The apparitions stopped visiting and the nightmares ceased immediately, but the next time he visited Fort Lauderdale, Dave returned to the Salvation Army.

"Remember the wooden masks you used to have?" he asked a man who appeared to be some sort of manager. "They've been sold," was his cold reply. "I know they've been sold, I'm the one who bought them," Dave explained. "I'm just trying to find out if you know anything about them, where they might have come from?"

The manager looked at him blankly for a moment. "There was a girl in here the other day who said she would do anything to get those masks back, and I mean anything."

What possesses the masks is anybody's guess. They may have been crafted with evil intent, or used by one of their previous owners in voodoo rituals. Perhaps they are a classic case of inanimate objects taking on the personalities of the dead, but we may never know. The masks are in a safe place, and Rob is having nothing but sweet dreams since the masks went away.

Perhaps it is another subtle warning from the spirit world. Be careful of the objects you possess, or one day they may end up possessing you.

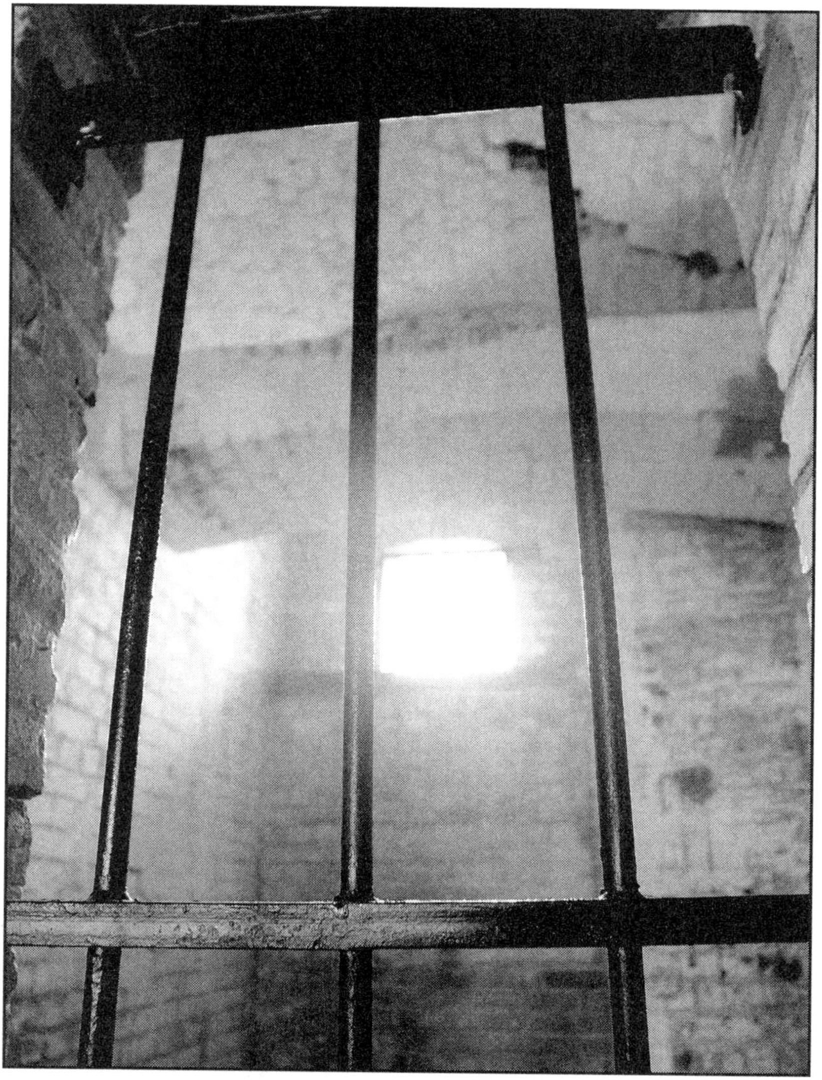

A cell in Fort Zachary Taylor.

Photo:roboneal.com

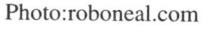

The Sentinel

While tourists relax on the beaches of Key West's state park, unsettled spirits rule Fort Zachary Taylor, still trapped in a time when the area was anything but paradise. "The Sentinel" is one woman's story of her unexpected encounter with one of the fort's many ghosts.

"**G**ive me some water," barked the raspy voice. His demand was a cross between uncontrollable anger and a plea for help driven with a tone that sent shivers down Abigail's spine. She jumped back, emitting a quiet yelp that drew the attention of her fellow tour mates. Following the voice to a desolate brick room west of the fort's parade grounds she saw an image that eluded the rest of the group, but would haunt her for months to come. There was an unkempt, sunburned man in uniform gripping his hands against the bars which turned the small room into a cell. Abigail looked back to the tour group and then the cell. He was gone.

Abigail was a regular in Key West. Born in Memphis, she first came to the Keys in 1982 for a veterinary convention, fell in love with the place and continued coming back two or three times a year. She was the first of her family to graduate college and the only to become a doctor, but Abigail inherited the family business none the less. She came from a family of psychics and saw ghosts from time to time but was unable to control when or why.

Fort Zachary Taylor was built soon after Florida became a state, with construction starting in 1845. The three-story fort was not completed until 1866 – the 21-year delay attributed to the remote location, shortages of men and supplies, the occasional hurricane and yellow fever epidemics. Though she gained notoriety in 1861 when occupied by the Union Army, making Key West the southernmost city under Yankee control, old Fort Taylor eventually outgrew her uses and in time had levels removed, areas remodeled, and sections filled. The area is known today as one of the best beaches in Key West, but includes sections of the fort that were restored with the help of a ghost. Abigail was unaware of the fort's haunted history until she spoke with the ranger who had guided her tour.

"What was the room used for that we passed by after entering the parade grounds?" she asked.

"The one you got spooked at?" Raymond replied. Abigail smiled and asked him what he knew.

"People talk about ghosts around here, but I don't really believe in that stuff," he said. "I've heard strange noises after the place closes and seen a few things, but we're out here on an island and it's probably just birds or shadows from the trees. The room you are wondering about was a holding cell. Not many prisoners passed through here, but they would have used the room to lock up soldiers who were drunk or disorderly."

Abigail plugged in her laptop that night and came across a Miami Herald article. It seems the fort was going to waste until Howard England, an engineer at the Naval Air Station, became curious about it in the 1970s. He began excavating in his free time and came across the largest collection of Civil War cannons in the nation. The antiquated weapons had been buried shortly before the Spanish-American War in order to strengthen the fort, but the more Howard found, the more he wanted to know. Howard told the Miami Herald:

"I used to try to figure out where things were in the excavation. Like for example, how was the desalinization plant laid out? I couldn't tell. Where would certain things be?"

"I would dream about it at night. It would go through your mind ñ you can't keep it out of your mind."

This is where the helpful ghost came in.

"It seemed to me one day I was in room 13. We were still about halfway down in the digging. I heard a voice say, 'What be you looking for Sonny?' I looked up and there was this man standing next to me in a Civil War uniform, with a white beard."

"I said, 'Well, I'm looking for guns and things.' He said, 'Well, it's here. That's old Betsy. That was my gun. This was my room.'"

When Howard resumed digging he found his first gun right where the spirit had told him. He was visited again and learned the location of the desalinization plant and eventually the soldier's name, which was Wendell Gardner.

Though Howard never researched the apparition who helped him excavate the fort, one day he was talking with a tourist fascinated by Key West and the Civil War.

"One of my ancestors served at this fort," the visitor said. "His name was Wendell Gardner."

Abigail returned to the fort the following day telling her boyfriend she wanted more sun. After a brief swim she grabbed a bottle of water from the snack bar and headed back to the parade grounds where she met a ranger named Randy.

"What do you know about ghosts around here?" she asked.

Randy was more than experienced with the fort's ghosts and shared stories from across the years with Abigail, ghosts whistling Dixie, re-enactors who disappear before your eyes, images in your peripheral vision and soldiers who walk right through you.

"I get the strongest sensation back by the old tidal toilets," he said.

They talked for a while before walking by the cell from which Abigail had heard the voice. "It may have been Lieutenant McClure who you saw," Randy explained. "He was charged with treason by the Union Army and locked up here ñ vowed in his journal that he would avenge the imprisonment. If they were asking for water, it's a good chance they suffered from yellow fever."

Upon closer inspection of the room Abigail found nothing. No desperate soldier, no sounds or sensations, just an empty cell. She thanked Randy for his input, but still questioned what was real and what she had imagined.

As she left the park, Abigail placed the remainder of her bottled water against the cell wall and began to walk away, convinced the entire episode had been imagined. Looking up towards the setting sun she walked in the direction of her bike, but was interrupted by a somewhat familiar raspy voice. "Thanks, lady."

The Lady In Blue

While tourists sip drinks in one of Key West's most visited bars, another spirit continues to roam the area. Is she just another lost soul, or is the lady in blue looking for more victims?

Capt. Tony's hanging tree.

Photo:roboneal.com

"The bar you see just across the road is Captain Tony's Saloon. It was built way back in 1851, and it is said that from 1852 until 1875 it served not only as a bar, but also as an ice house and the city morgue." Patrick was entranced and stood close to Mattey as he told the story.

Patrick had recently turned 6 and was excited to visit Key West for the first time. Unfortunately his idea of fun was a little different than his mother's and Aunt Lindsay's, and after the second day of shopping on Duval Street he started looking for his own entertainment. As they passed the La Concha Hotel Patrick noticed a picture of a ghost and his eyes lit up. "Let's go on the Ghost Tour!" he exclaimed. Kathy and Lindsay's idea of fun was a little different than Patrick's this time.

But, the three went into the lobby where a man named Frank gave them all the information they needed. Patrick wanted to tour that night, but the ladies vetoed his decision in favor of a sunset cruise. "Give it a couple of days and he will forget all about it," Kathy kept saying. Patrick didn't forget.

"Are we going on the Ghost Tour tonight?" He asked the question several times a day, picking up brochures everywhere they went until finally the ladies gave in. They joined the tour the following night, and though skeptical at first, Kathy found herself wanting more as Mattey continued telling tales at the final stop of the evening.

"And if you take a look just above the roof of Captain Tony's you will see what looks like a tree," Mattey continued. "If you look carefully you will notice that the tree grows right up through the ceiling of the bar, and the reason they don't cut it down is because that is the original city hanging tree."

Patrick's eyes grew wider. He had seen that very tree earlier in the day.

"One unfortunate victim of the hanging tree still haunts the bar, and is known as the lady in blue. Back in the day, Key West was a pretty tight-knit community, but it seems this lady had a few prob-

41

lems and one night murdered her husband and her two children. Pretty brutal story, and some accounts even have her chopping them up into little pieces before retiring for the night. The town folk did not take too kindly to murder and as word spread about the crime, a lynch mob was formed to bring justice."

"It was just before dawn when they burst into the murderer's house and ripped her from the bed. The group marched her, clad only in a blue nightgown, down to the hanging tree where a noose was placed around her neck. Are all of you familiar with a noose?" The crowd nodded their heads as Mattey continued his account.

"The knot of the noose serves two purposes. One is to create a loop so that the person doesn't slip away, but the other purpose is to crack the victim's neck so they die a little quicker. This lady's neck didn't break and she was strangled to death by the tension. It is said that as the life drained from her body, her face turned the same color blue as her nightgown. She haunts the bar to this very day."

For reasons we don't really understand, she is most often seen in the ladies bathroom." Patrick's face turned white and a small damp patch appeared on the front of his pants before trickling down his leg and forming a puddle on the Greene Street sidewalk below. The young boy's eyes grew wide and his entire body shook as if he were going into seizures. Mattey stopped mid sentence, simultaneously walking towards the boy and dialing 911 from his cell phone.

"It's okay, don't worry," Mattey continued towards the boy as the voice spoke again. "It's okay, don't worry." It was Patrick's mom speaking as she picked up her son and walked to the rear of the tour group. Mattey tried to follow and make sure everything was alright but stopped short when a hand tugged his cape. "I'm his aunt. I'll explain everything when the Ghost Tour is over."

Mattey continued the story and answered questions when the tour was over. Nobody was leaving without hearing what was wrong with the boy, so Lindsay stepped up beside Mattey to explain with a little encouragement from the crowd.

"We've been trying to avoid the tour all week, but Patrick kept

pestering us. Yesterday we were walking by Captain Tony's when he spotted a skeleton behind the bar so we went in for a soda and took a look around. My sister, Patrick's mom, decided to use the bathroom before we left, so I watched Patrick and then decided to go myself. Patrick decided he should go too, but we didn't want him going into the men's room alone. It's not like he still needs help going to the bathroom, we just didn't know who might be in there, and the ladies room was empty so we sent him there while we watched the door."

"Patrick had had ghosts on the brain, so it didn't surprise us when he came out of the bathroom and said he was hearing voices. He kept talking about the lady in the bathroom that was trying to scare him. 'What did she say to you honey?' his mom asked.

'She said to get out and that she doesn't like me.'

'But no one is in the bathroom. Me and Aunt Lindsay were just in there and it's empty.'

'She said she wanted to cut me.'

The crowd went silent when Lindsay shared this part of the story and even the skeptics had a shocked look on their faces. Most of the group headed in to Captain Tony's for a drink, but not one of them dared to use the ladies room that night.

US Highway 1.

Photo:roboneal.com

The Ghost of U.S.1

While thousands of tourists effortlessly travel the length of highway U.S.1 from Miami to Key West, there are those who encounter trouble. Some are not so fortunate, but others receive a helping hand from the ghost of U.S.1.

She began to panic. Heavy gusts of rain assaulted the windshield with an intensity even the fastest wipers could not battle. The black-top road and pitch-dark sky blended seamlessly and frequent bolts of lightning provided the only means of navigation. "Oh my god, I think I am going to die!"

Tammy Sigman came to Key West from Plano, Texas eight months after her husband passed away. It had been a difficult year with the children and the Southernmost City seemed like an ideal place to enjoy a week of sun and fun while leaving her troubles back home. The trip got off to a terrible start. The taxi that was to take her to the airport arrived late, she missed her first flight, and upon arriving at Miami International Airport discovered her rental car was no longer available. "At least they didn't lose my bags," she thought to herself.

The rental car situation worked out when one became available in Fort Lauderdale, but it was almost midnight by the time Tammy hit the road. She was tired, cranky and like so many other tourists had no idea it would take four more hours to reach Key West. "What else can go wrong?" she wondered. Then it started to rain.

U.S.1 is breathtaking the first few times you see it. Like anything else, the novelty wears off when you drive it on a regular basis and after a few years of living in the Keys, you start to realize what a dangerous road it can be. A single lane in each direction, visitors driving slow to enjoy the views, locals getting agitated and trying to pass, drunk drivers, deer in the roadway, poor lighting and tropical weather can all spell disaster. For Tammy, it started with the rain.

It was a light sprinkle at first, but picked up with intensity. She twisted the plastic knob in her rented Hyundai adjusting the wiper speed from low to medium and eventually high, then turned down the radio before gripping both hands tightly around the wheel. Fiddling with the defroster only made things worse and panic set in.

"Just great!" she spoke aloud this time to no one in particular. "Here I am a single mom stuck in a monsoon in the middle of

nowhere, water on both sides of the road and a piece of junk rental car that won't even defrost right. Damn it!" Her first thought was of pulling to the side of the road, but in order to execute this maneuver she needed to see where the side of the road was. The blinding rain made it impossible to tell where the cement became sand or where the sand became water. Stopping seemed like a bad idea as well. "What if someone else can't see and plows me from behind?" She turned off the radio and nearly broke the turn signal trying to get more speed out of the wipers. The storm's force increased and she found her nose just inches from the windshield in a futile effort to make out the lines of the road. "Somebody please help me," she begged, though no one else was in the car. At that moment taillights appeared on the road in front of her.

Tammy felt a hint of comfort knowing she was not the only one caught in this mess, and judging by the steadiness of the other vehicle, they were not having the same problems with defrosters, windshield wipers and navigation. The red lights emitted a soothing glow that cast down on the yellow dividing line. As she grew more comfortable with the situation the lead car gradually increased its speed and Tammy soon found that the storm was beginning to dissipate.

The mini convoy went on for twenty minutes before the rain was reduced to a sprinkle. Tammy wondered about the best way to thank her new friend and hedged between stopping them for drinks or just passing by with a friendly honk and a hearty wave. A wave seemed like the most logical thing to do. "They might not even realize that they saved my life." She switched the wipers back to low and glanced down at the radio turning it on at a low volume. When she looked back to the road ahead of her the car was gone.

"What the...? How did they disappear so quickly? Where did they go? Where could they go?" Tammy increased her speed in hopes of catching up to say thanks, but the road ahead was empty. No turnoffs, no restaurants or shops, just a two-lane highway with water on every side.

Tammy's vacation took a turn for the better and she soon made

Key West a regular get away, returning several times a year, but flying directly into Key West each time. One evening she met a couple at Mallory Square and the conversation turned to the terrible storm they encountered on the drive down. No visibility, unable to see the road, fearful of going into the ocean, a pair of red taillights and a mystery car that led them safely through the storm.

As the couple explained their brush with death a chill shot down Tammy's spine. "The car was there one second and gone the next," Greg explained. "It was the middle of the afternoon and there was nowhere it could have gone, so we pulled into a little bait shop and asked the old man if there were any other roads. He was a bit reserved at first, but when we told him about what happened he seemed to get a bit choked up and then just smiled at us. 'Looks like you got a little help from the ghost of U.S.1.'"

Fatalities on the highway from Florida City to Key West increase every year. Twenty-five people lost their lives in 1999, twenty-seven in 2000, twenty-nine in 2001 and 30 in 2002. Legend has it that at least one of the highway's victims is still doing their part to make sure everyone who visits the Keys has a safe vacation.

The Séance

While most people are content waiting for the spirits to come to them, others prefer to seek them out. "The Séance" describes this author's first-hand experience with the mystical practice in an Old Town guest house.

Seance

Photo: roboneal.com

Twelve people crowded into the Old Town guest room preparing to join hands and attempt to contact the spirit world. While some were unable to conceal their nervousness, most of the participants had a gleam of excitement in their eyes. I looked at the situation with a mixture of hopefulness and skepticism. I was number thirteen.

Ghosts have been my passion ever since Mrs. Ubercedar thrilled our kindergarten class with tales of a Native American spirit who lived behind the walls of her 18th century Pennsylvania home. I was hooked after she showed us an actual photograph of the ghost, and after two decades of reading everything paranormal I could get my hands on, I was fortunate enough to convert my passion into one of the best jobs in the world ñ telling ghost stories in Key West.

I was always a believer, but with this transition came an obligation to look at situations from a skeptic's point of view. At present I believe that ghosts most definitely exist in our world, but in many cases the things we believe to be ghostly in nature can be explained by science or attributed to an overactive imagination. I guess you could say I am a believer who looks for other options.

I don't like Ouija Boards and subscribe to the general belief that they can invite unwanted spirits. Over the years I have turned down many an invitation to attempt contact with the other side using such a board, but when an opportunity to join a séance in one of Key West's most haunted homes arose, it was just too good an opportunity to pass up.

The home was typical of those found in Old Town. It was a two-story, wooden structure built in the late 1800s and accented with wraparound balconies and pastel shutters. Two guests were waiting outside the etched glass door as I approached. The door slowly opened to reveal a man named Simon.

"Good evening," he said with a staged Romanian accent straight out of a bad horror movie. There was a smile in his eyes as he led us up the staircase to the second floor. As the stairs creaked beneath our feet, Simon introduced himself to Emily and Ernest. They were hon-

eymooners from Virginia and had been invited by a palm reader they met just a few hours before. Simon and I needed no introduction as I had met him a number of times in the past while researching the ghosts that resided in his house.

He took us to the room where the others had gathered and my eyes glanced across the walls and ceiling looking for any signs of trickery. I recalled that this was one of the bedrooms, though the furniture had been removed for the seance, and all that was left to show it had been lived in was a small fringed table lamp and an Oriental carpet that sprawled the length of the floor.

Directly across the room was a staircase that spiraled up to a smaller bedroom with a widow's walk above. Measuring no more than eight feet in diameter, the quaint room was surrounded by windows on all sides and made up the only section of the house at the third-floor level. Some would call the room charming, but the charm faded rapidly as the night went on.

Introductions were made and brief conversations filled the room helping to ease some of the tension. A tall man with flowing brown hair and milky blue eyes that were almost transparent asked that everyone be seated on the floor, side by side, so as to create a circle. Beside him were the different items to assist in welcoming the spirits and a small leather satchel with a black woven drawstring. Jay was a warlock and would be leading the séance.

The lights suddenly went out and the room was filled with a collective anxiety, much like people experience when a plane hits turbulence without warning. It was only Renee, turning off the switch of the table lamp. Excitement replaced fear as she lit a white candle that sent shadows dancing across the faces of everyone in the circle. Renee was a psychic in town and had joined the séance to act as a median ñ she would be the voice if any of the spirits wished to speak.

Jay spoke first, explaining the purpose of the séance and offering a prayer of protection to keep any evil spirits away. One by one he placed items on the table, explaining the purpose of each as he went along.

"The white candle represents fire. Fire can be used as a great tool, but it must also be respected or it can easily destroy. Keep your eyes on the flame as the spirits may use it to indicate their presence."

Incense was burned to represent the wind, a small vial of water was placed in the circle and the small leather satchel was revealed to contain soil from the ground to signify earth. With all four elements in place we joined hands and the spirits were summoned.

The candle flickered; some people felt a slight chill and Ernest even claimed to have the vision of a woman playing piano. Though no one would be proud to admit they had failed in their attempts to contact the spirit world, I could not help but think that I had just spent the last half hour sitting on an uncomfortable floor with nothing to show for it but two sweaty hands.

The lights were turned back on and we began discussing what we had or had not experienced when I noticed something out of the corner of my eye. It was a quick movement that I first thought was a person peeking down the staircase, but when I turned to look it was gone. Nothing strange about this, but a few seconds later it happened again. Once more I turned my head and nothing was there.

I never suspected ghosts, but the object continued to evade my peripheral vision and was becoming quite annoying. After several minutes of attempting to determine the source, I asked Simon if I could have a look upstairs. He was happy to oblige.

Beginning my ascent, I looked to the top of the staircase expecting to find a ceiling fan that had been casting the odd shadow. As I hit the third step my gaze continued upwards but I was stopped dead in my tracks as my face, chest and knee hit the equivalent of a brick wall. Nothing was visible but I was physically prevented from moving forward. A dense heat enveloped my entire body causing my heart to beat faster than I ever imagined it could. I stood motionless for a moment and then heeded the advice of a little voice in my head. "Turn around and go down. Turn around and go down. Turn around and go down."

Jay gave me a curious glance as I stepped silently back into the

room. "Why didn't you go up?" he asked.

The last thing I'm going to tell someone after holding a séance is that I was unable to ascend the staircase due to some supernatural force field that no one can see, so I decided to give myself a little reality check. "Why don't you give it a try?" I replied.

Jay began his ascent but was stopped in the same manner as he attempted to reach the fourth step. He turned and smiled before saying, "Something doesn't want us up there. Why don't we try it together?"

I joined Jay's side on the stairs and we both attempted to reach the top. There was a strong tension at first, but we were able to move forward one step at a time. The tension felt like we were pushing our weight against a giant balloon but the tension broke when we reached the top step and our surroundings became very surreal.

There was a strange calm about the room when we first entered but it was rapidly replaced by chaos and the space was filled with thousands of small gray objects that flew about the room. "Bats," I thought, but this was something very different. They were dark in color and consistent in size, but their shapes were constantly changing as they shot across the room in every direction. It seemed strange that we were untouched by the creatures as they flew about so erratically, but even stranger when we realized they were going right through us.

Jay and I stared blankly at each other. There was so much confusion that fear had no time to set in. I had the feeling that time was standing still as the gray streaks continued to swoop around us in silence, but the silence was broken by a shrill scream.

"No! Stop It! Get Out! Leave!" It was Renee screaming from the room below. Jay and I rushed down the stairs as the bizarre whisps escaped through closed windows by the hundreds. When we reached Renee she was shaking. "I don't know what that was, but I have never felt something so strong in all of my life. I've got to get out of here." Everyone left uncertain about what had just happened.

Three years passed and I learned to keep the story to myself as most people found it less than believable. One night the story resur-

faced when I was talking to a median who stuck around to chat after the tour.

"There are many spirits that wish to make contact from the other side," she explained. "When you hold a séance these spirits will gather above in hopes of being called upon. Look at the séance as a doctor's office and the area directly above it as a waiting room. Though the séance was over, many of the spirits were still in the waiting room hoping they may be called. When you penetrated the protective bubble you entered the waiting room of the spirit world."

It was the last séance I ever attended.

About the Author

David L. Sloan is the President and Founder of Key West's Original Ghost Tour and Phantom Press. He resides in Florida with his cat Dr. Jeckyll and bird T.J.

Sloan is the author of *Ghosts of Key West* and *Quit Your Job and Move To Key West*. He is terrible at responding to e-mails but can be reached at david@phantompress.com.